CHATTANOOGA
LANDMARKS

To Jim,
I hope these stories
guide you to lots of
adventures in
Chattanooga's history.

A panorama of Moccasin Bend, this view from Lookout Mountain shows the shape that gave the area, settled during the Paleo-Indian Period, its name.

CHATTANOOGA
LANDMARKS

EXPLORING THE HISTORY
OF THE SCENIC CITY

JENNIFER CRUTCHFIELD

Charleston London

THE
History
PRESS

Published by The History Press

Charleston, SC 29403
www.historypress.net

First published 2010

Manufactured in the United States

ISBN 978.1.59629.447.9

Library of Congress Cataloging-in-Publication Data

Crutchfield, Jennifer.
Chattanooga landmarks : exploring the history of the scenic city / Jennifer Crutchfield.
p. cm.
ISBN 978-1-59629-447-9
1. Chattanooga (Tenn.)--History. 2. Historic sites--Tennessee--Chattanooga. 3. Historic
buildings--Tennessee--Chattanooga. 4. Chattanooga (Tenn.)--Buildings, structures, etc. 5.
Chattanooga (Tenn.)--Antiquities. 6. Chattanooga (Tenn.)--Description and travel. I. Title.
F444.C457C78 2010
976.8'82--dc22
2010031976

This book is dedicated to the families who turned their hope into Chattanooga's future and to those who will take our history and weave it into new generations. Personally, I dedicate my efforts to my children and to the families, friends and loved ones who have guided us. The Ley, Crutchfield, Hailey, McDonald and Maguire families have endowed us with love, safety, self-worth, belonging and history, the recipe for building a future by understanding the past.

Professionally, I would like to thank Mai Bell Hurley, Michael Kull, Allison Gorman, the Regional History staff at the Chattanooga–Hamilton County Bicentennial Library, Cornerstones, the Chattanooga History Center, The History Press and all of the professionals who help us serve Chattanooga families through the Chattanooga Parent Magazine. As a lifelong learner, I owe a debt of gratitude to Zella Armstrong, Dr. James W. Livingood, Robert Sparks Walker, Jac Chambliss, Max Bahner, John Wilson, Dean Arnold, Maury Nicely and the other men and women who have found passion in the history of their city, the Scenic City.

CONTENTS

CONTENTS

Contents

INTRODUCTION

C hattanooga has charmed people since its first visitors broke through the wilderness, and their marvels, innovations and civic achievements have reflected the progress, advances and achievements of the country. The progress of ancient man from Paleo-Indian to the abilities and advances attributed to the Mississippian Period can be seen at Moccasin Bend and Williams Island in the longest contiguous prehistoric sites in the Southeast, documenting those social, political and technological changes.

As Chattanooga goes, so has gone the country, and the rebirth and revitalization of post–Civil War Chattanooga was a model for a country struggling with the physical and emotional scars of a bloody war. The "Dynamo of Dixie" became an industrial icon as the city on the Tennessee River supplied the industries that powered the country's rebirth. When Chattanooga struggled to fight the pollution that their industrial advances brought, the nation watched.

Remarkable innovations, explorations and migrations have touched the Scenic City, and their marks remain on the landmarks, geologic marvels and buildings embraced by the people who remember the past and celebrated by the ones who look toward the hopeful, bright future of a city that is more than scenic. Chattanoogans have never been known to run from a challenge, instead embracing the opportunity to overcome obstacles. The history of the people and their places is a moving story of change, hope and progress set in a land that is rich with the glory of nature.

This colorful Cherokee maiden was the cover image of one of Adolph Och's special editions of the *Chattanooga Times*, circa 1892.

Chapter 1

FROM ROSS'S LANDING TO THE MOUNTAIN

Ross's Landing

In 1816, travelers must have felt like they were coming out of the wilderness when their riverboats landed at a shanty collection of buildings at a trading post called Ross's Landing. Supplying the riverboats and barges that carried pioneers on the ever-moving trek westward, the community that sprung up in the peaceful bend of the river was also called Ross's Warehouse for the massive amount of supplies that waited there for the journey toward westward expansion.

Since the Old French Store on Williams Island became the first white settlement in 1769, the community became the center of cultural and educational life of the Cherokee, linking Ross's Landing to the family business farther inland in Georgia. The sixteenth state to enter the Union in 1796, Tennessee formed Hamilton County in October 1819 from lands ceded in the 1817 Hiwassee Purchase from the Cherokee.

John and his father, Daniel Ross, were a magnificent combination of Scottish and Cherokee qualities, their teamwork, community leadership and kinship making their trading posts regular stops along the Great Warpath and Trading Path that traversed the Tennessee River Valley. The terms of the Hiwassee Purchase Treaty of 1817 called for the Cherokee tribe to cede a large portion of land for the formation of the territory to be called Hamilton County.

Daniel Ross must have been a most remarkable man. He left his native Scotland for the New World when he was a boy, and as a twenty-five-year-

The son of Scottish trader Daniel Ross, Chief John Ross led the Cherokee Nation during the critical time leading up to the Trail of Tears.

old man, he was venturing south to begin a trading enterprise, bound for Chickasaw territory. Bloody Fellow, chief of the Tuskegee Island area we call Williams Island, stopped the trading party at the mouth of Citico Creek.

As Chief Bloody Fellow weighed the gain to be had from killing the Chickasaws and their Scottish trader, another Chattanooga legend arrived, sent by a messenger to offer Bloody Fellow counsel. John McDonald, another Scottish trader, had come to the Indian territory acting as an agent for the British and as a trader serving both supplier and customer.

McDonald persuaded Ross to join him as a trader in the Cherokee territory, and the following year the young trader married McDonald's daughter Mollie. Their son, John Ross, would grow to lead his nation, leaving a legacy that is still celebrated at the shores of the Tennessee River.

Today's Ross's Landing booms yearly with Riverbend, a nine-day musical celebration that began thirty years ago as Five Nights, now featuring more than one hundred artists on the same land that once resonated with the sounds of building, growth, sorrow and war. The dim sounds of padding feet and worn, tired moccasins might be imagined in the gurgling sounds of the path that honors their memory, a testament to the tribes moved west during the Trail of Tears. The Passage commemorates those early Americans, and at the trailhead for the 1838 removal, today's visitors can enjoy a pedestrian connection that links the Tennessee Aquarium to the river with cascading fountains and Cherokee art, happy children a stark contrast to the workers at the Bluff Furnace when it was home to the East Tennessee Iron Manufacturing Company chartered by Robert Cravens in 1847.

In August 1863, Union soldiers stationed on the ridge opposite this site under General William Rosecrans began shelling the city and Confederate positions on the Tennessee River near the shore, and Union forces crossed here to begin their advances on the city.

BRAINERD MISSION

The Brainerd Mission was opened in the early 1800s, near where Eastgate Mall is now. Missionaries operated a church there for the many Cherokee Indians who lived in the area. In fact, the Cherokee grandmother of Chief

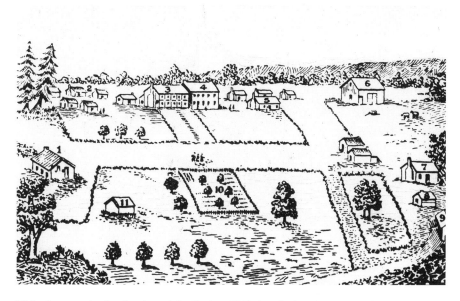

This photograph of a drawing of the Brainerd Mission depicts the community established by the American Board of Foreign Missions to educate the Cherokee people.

John Ross (who founded Ross's Landing downtown) is buried in the church's cemetery, right across from the China Moon Restaurant.

The very last church service at the Brainerd Mission must have been emotional. It was late summer 1838, and the Cherokee were being forced by the government to leave the Chattanooga area for good. They were beginning a long journey west called the Trail of Tears. Most of the missionaries who worked with the Cherokee vowed to go with them. Try to picture the pride with which they used their Communion set. It was more than seven hundred years old and must have been a valued gift to a congregation that had forged a community out of a wilderness.

Many of the travelers did not survive the difficult journey at all, and several of the missionaries got very sick and had to return to Chattanooga. Among those returning were John Vail and Ainsworth Blunt, who used the Communion set when they started First Presbyterian, one of the first churches in town.

The Communion set later traveled to Dalton, Georgia, when Ainsworth Blunt spread his mission to that untamed wilderness region. (Have you ever been to Dalton or Brainerd? Can you imagine either one of them as "untamed wilderness"?)

The Brainerd Mission Communion set served the First Presbyterian Church when a missionary who fell ill during the Trail of Tears returned to Chattanooga.

The Brainerd Mission Communion set was already nine hundred years old when it was given to Ainsworth Blunt for use in celebrating Christianity with the Cherokee.

The Missing Treasures

In 1930, Lizzie Kirby, the daughter of Ainsworth Blunt, was an elderly woman living in Dalton. She loaned her father's Communion set to Chattanooga's First Presbyterian Church to use in its anniversary celebrations. The set was not returned but was featured in newspaper accounts of area events during the next few decades. The current location of the set is not publicly known.

In 2001, a boy named John Wright, an Eagle Scout, began working with his dad on a revitalization project at the mission. Jack Wright, a retired safety engineer from McKee Bakery, became enthralled with the mystery. After a lot of detective work, he found out where the Communion set was being kept. He even got pictures of it! But he was sworn to secrecy. Later, while traveling home with his wife from a tour of the western sites of the Trail of Tears, Jack Wright had a heart attack and died. The secret may be buried with him.

Where did the treasure go?

This present-day photograph of the Brainerd Mission Communion set was taken at an unknown location after a historic search by a Chattanooga Eagle Scout and his father.

A TIMELINE FOR THE BRAINERD MISSION COMMUNION SET

1087–1100	Communion set made in England during the reign of William Rufus, King of England
1822	Given to the Brainerd Mission
1838	Used in final service before the mission was closed for the Trail of Tears
1840	Ainsworth Blunt started First Presbyterian
1847	Ainsworth Blunt started Dalton Presbyterian
1865	Set no longer used by church and given to Blunt's daughter, Lizzie Kirby
1930	Lizzie Kirby loaned set to First Presbyterian for 90-year anniversary
1954	Set on display at Pioneer Bank opening on Brainerd Road*
1965	Set used at Daughters of the American Revolution Silver Tea honoring the Brainerd Mission*
2001	Eagle Scout John Wright III and his father obtain current photographs of Brainerd set

* *Chattanooga Times*

Underground Chattanooga

In 1978, rumors began to swirl about strange things being found in some buildings in downtown Chattanooga. Utility workers whispered to one another about stairs leading to nowhere, ground-height windows, barred doors, empty rooms, bricked-up archways and other architectural oddities. Something lay under the streets of downtown. But what?

The mystery of underground Chattanooga was solved—not by official detectives but by utility workers and archaeologists, regular people who asked questions and found answers.

Dr. Jeff Brown, a professor of archaeology at the University of Tennessee at Chattanooga, was fascinated by the steps that led to nowhere. He helped solve the mystery by using something you've probably heard about in school: the scientific method.

Here's what he discovered. Before there were dams to help control the Tennessee River, Chattanooga suffered ferocious floods. One flood in particular—the flood of 1867—is said to have been devastating, the worst in the city's history. The damage was so bad that people in Chattanooga decided there was only one thing to do: make downtown higher!

The people of Chattanooga helped city workers. They used whatever fill was available to shore up empty lots, basements and parts of streets. By

Warner Park, now home to the Chattanooga Zoo and a water feature, is seen in this 1917 photo of one of the last great floods to befall Chattanooga.

1890, residents and city workers had raised some streets in the downtown flood zone by two to nine feet. The landscape of entire blocks was changed as Chattanoogans battled the ravages of Mother Nature and fought floodwaters.

Some of the downtown buildings we see now sit right on top of what used to be the first-floor rooms of older buildings. Those rooms are still there—but now they're underground. Today, sharp "investigators" can still recognize the hidden signs of underground Chattanooga.

MARKET STREET BRIDGE

Like a "huge monster of primeval days," according to the *Chattanooga Times*, the bridge over the Tennessee River at Market Street has enthralled Chattanoogans since its construction began in late 1914. This 2,675-foot-long bridge has a span of 300 feet.

The Market Street Bridge, known also as the Chief John Ross Bridge, celebrates the legendary role that Chief John Ross played in the community that started as Ross's Landing.

From Ross's Landing to the Mountain

Children and adults alike have gaped with wonder on the rare occasions that the bridge has been opened, its mechanical perfection seeming strange and mysterious. A member of the original bridge team had previously worked on another modern marvel, the Panama Canal.

The Market Street Bridge features four arch spans of 180 feet each and a channel span of 300 feet, and the bascule span required 2.7 million pounds of structural steel. Another 1.9 million pounds of steel reinforcing bars maintain the structural integrity of this behemoth structure. The rolling-lift bascule bridge uses enormous, concrete counterweights weighing 3,600 tons and made with 1,502 cubic yards of concrete.

This bridge, which has graced the Chattanooga skyline for generations, was considered the "greatest concrete bridge in the South." Certainly it was a far cry from the first wooden bridge built at the site by the Union army in 1864.

The Meigs Military Bridge replaced the pontoon bridges, and built in 1865, the Union project earned the nickname "Meigs Folly" for its $75,000 price tag. A one-thousand-foot wooden-plank bridge, it was washed away in the 1867 flood, much to the relief of the townspeople, for whom it had become a dangerous burden.

Mayhem on Market Street

Torrential floods raged through the Tennessee Valley in the winter of 1915, when the Market Street Bridge was one year into its three-year construction. Brave men worked through the night to keep powerful accumulations of driftwood from toppling the new bridge's 180-foot-high frameworks.

By dawn, ice was beginning to form around these courageous men; finally, when the huge structure of steel and timber crashed, the noise was said to have sounded like the retorts of hundreds of guns.

A tugboat gave chase, and as the thirty-two-foot flood raged around them, the crew roped the floating mass of steel and wood, catching it in the bend around Williams Island. The bravery of the men on that cold winter night was just another marvel in the building of what's been called the South's greatest bridge.

Mystery in the Morning

At 10:30 a.m. on April 7, 1950, a taxi driver, a housewife and a man in a Buick convertible—all driving across the Market Street Bridge—scrambled as each of their cars screeched, rolled and was tossed like a toy by the massive power of the bridge, which had unexpectedly opened beneath them.

Heralded for its innovative engineering, the Market Street Bridge seldom opens. This photograph depicts an accidental opening in the early 1900s.

It was determined that there was no power to the motor to initiate the bridge's opening, so the accident couldn't have been the result of a "tripped lever." A more likely theory is that the span's massive counterweights may not have been balanced, and the powerful jarring of the surprise release caused the gears to become unmeshed.

A cry went out for help, and it was answered by businesses all over town. A massive, ad hoc team of Chattanoogans used jacks and machinery to raise the counterweight enough to put the gears back into place. In the end, all three drivers were brought down safely.

Robert Twomey was a contractor with the Service Electric Company working on the bridge during that crisis; his son and namesake has fond memories of the experience his father had working on the Market Street Bridge. And in the kind of irony seemingly "made in Chattanooga," the younger Robert Twomey built the podium from which our current mayor guides the city today.

WALNUT STREET BRIDGE

The opening of the Walnut Street Bridge was an event celebrated on both sides of the river. Its construction had been a dream since 1882, when the mayor and civil leadership began lobbying Washington, D.C., for construction support. Since the failed Meigs Bridge during the Civil War, often noted as Meigs Folly in photographs, residents of the ever-growing Hill City community depended on the ferry for access across the Tennessee River.

Hamilton County sold $200,000 in 5 percent bonds to support the construction of the bridge, with another $25,000 contributed by the Hill City citizens. John B. Neely was awarded the contract to supervise the construction. The native of Virginia was both a Confederate veteran and the man who supervised the building of much of the Cincinnati Southern Railroad. Also a former director of the Dixie Powder Company, a boat was kept handy for Neely because he had a propensity to fall off the barge in his enthusiasm to correct problems during the construction of the bridge.

Edward Betts, an integral assistant during the building phase, received an emergency call one afternoon. His co-workers watched as he hurriedly grabbed the scales used to weigh building materials and rushed home to answer his wife's emergency: weighing their new son Clarence on the Walnut Street Bridge's scales. Completed in 1891, the 2,730-foot bridge is the longest pedestrian bridge in the world and is the oldest surviving truss bridge.

When the bridge fell into disrepair and was threatened with demolition, the machine of revitalization's gears ground until a public-private partnership raised funds to save the bridge, converting it into the longest pedestrian bridge in the county, another testament to the commitment to quality of life that Chattanoogans hold dear. Plaques were sold to raise the funds for the rehabilitation of the bridge. Now, many of those same families, together with their new generations, walk across the Tennessee River, enjoying the breezes, views and fellowship that characterize progress in the Scenic City.

MACLELLAN ISLAND

There is a wild, lush, wooded 18.8 acres in the middle of the Tennessee River that exist today very much like they must have been since the last ice age, when modern man began walking in our valley. Maclellan Island has been the site of archaeological digs producing relics that date man's history on that island back to twelve to fifteen thousand years ago. Gorges and remains revealed by floodwaters gave evidence to sites from the Paleo-Indian Period (circa 14000–8000 BC), the Archaic and Mississippian Periods (circa 1500–1335 BC) and the Woodland Period (circa 405 BC).

The Cherokee, following the tradition of their "Long Man," chose sites on the banks of flowing water and in the valleys of majestic mountains. Their history is etched in the land, seasoned with the flavor of Hernando de Soto's soldiers who traveled from Chattanooga to Guntersville, Alabama, in 1540. The French merchants used the gorge, Tennessee's Grand Canyon, as a trade route from Mississippi to Charleston, South Carolina, and made their mark on the valley in the 1600s.

Then the land was dominated by warring tribes and visited by hapless pioneers. Victims of the powerful, raging 8.5-mile stretch's dangers called Tumbling Shoals with the Suck, the Skillet, the Kettle, the Pan, the Pot, the Frying Pan and the Boiling Pot, the brave travelers who survived were wary of the screams of warriors, bloodthirsty and vengeful. The hardwood trees, vines, river cane and wildflowers of Maclellan Island were also refuge in another time for runaway slaves, free hearts traveling on an Underground Railroad to a land with neighbors who called them brother and equal.

Visitors to the island today, travelers, children and Chattanoogans alike, can see a natural anomaly not present during the land's history: a rain shadow desert. The phenomenon of rain shadow deserts are normally seen in areas that lie in the shadows of mountain ranges, receiving little precipitation. Some of the most famous examples are Death Valley in the shadow of the Sierra Nevada, the Patagonian and Monte Deserts in Argentina and deserts formed in the lee side of Chile's famous mountain range, the Andes. As air ascends on one side of a range, it releases the moisture that it is carrying, descending dry on the lee side. In sight of the mountain receiving the rainfall, a desert forms in its shadow.

Veteran's Bridge is the widest of the four bridges that cross the Tennessee River, connecting Georgia Avenue downtown to Barton Avenue and Hixson Pike in the north shore with a steel girder structure. It was built in 1984 with a main span of 420 feet. Its shadow created a narrow strip of rain shadow desert on Maclellan Island, a lush haven for flora and an aviary haven made possible by the Audubon Society and the generosity of a man with an eye to the future.

Robert J. Maclellan, known affectionately to his friends as Bob, was the son of a devout, prescient and inspirational Presbyterian named Thomas Maclellan. Thomas was a zealous man, his faith so strong that he is said to have made a covenant with God before moving his home from Scotland to Chattanooga. He founded Provident Insurance, known now as UnumProvident Corporation, the largest disability insurance firm in the nation. His faith and spirit resound in the works of his progeny through, among other efforts, the Maclellan Foundation. The family's charitable giving has supported the McCallie School, the Chattanooga Christian School and character education in public schools, and in 1954, Robert J. Maclellan gave the island in the downstream third of the Tennessee River to the Audubon Society so that it might be preserved and shared.

Bob Maclellan was one of eight men who were colloquially referred to as the "Guinea Table," men who met and shared discussion, fellowship and ideas for the future at the iconic Chattanooga club, the Mountain City Club. Leaders in their families, community and corporations, these men were protective of their city, philanthropic but also fearful, worried that too much progress might hurt their businesses and the local economy that depended on them. Local legend says that their sons and daughters called for progress, and its fruit can be seen in the changed landscape of the city.

Chattanooga Venture is at the heart of Ross's Landing and the aquarium. The revitalization spreads from the riverfront to the creative collectives on the emerging Southside and Main Street to the energy that jumps over the bridges to gentrify the Northshore communities, bolstered by the frolic and fresh beauty of Coolidge Park and the dynamic spirit of Frazier Avenue.

The skies were gray and the future was bright in 1984 when these visionary leaders of Chattanooga Venture called their neighbors to join them in Vision 2000, a public participation program designed to give citizens a voice in the changes in their community and its future. Vision 2000 involved over 1,700 people and is lauded around the country as one of the first and most successful examples of public-private partnerships working toward a visionary goal. New generations of Chattanoogans continue the work of these hardworking philanthropists, organizers and community leaders who toiled alongside mothers, laborers and citizens of all kinds.

Today, Chattanoogans can also enjoy the wonders of Tennessee's Grand Canyon aboard the aquarium's new River Gorge Explorer, touring some of the sixteen thousand acres of land protected by the Tennessee River Gorge Trust. This land is home to one thousand varieties of plants and hundreds of animal species and was established in 1981.

Seaworthy travelers can board one of the Chattanooga Ducks, authentic World War II amphibious vehicles, and go from shore to the boat dock on the downstream end of Maclellan Island in the same seat. A two-mile hiking trail loops around the perimeter of the 18.8-acre island, and on the upstream end, a blue heron rookery offers an observation platform and the opportunity to observe a nesting area and a colony in action. The Chattanooga Water Taxi also offers a holiday excursion, with Santa's Helpers frolicking in the aviary paradise that has seen Chattanoogans come and go for thousands of years.

BLUFF VIEW ARTS DISTRICT

Mansions lining the impressive Bluff cliffs above the Tennessee River changed from a residential neighborhood to a destination arts district, the impetus created by the Hunter Museum igniting a renewed revitalization led by Dr. and Mrs. Charles "Tony" Portera. The two-acre Bluff View Sculpture Garden was the gift of Chattanoogan Scott L. Probasco and complemented the change as mansions became restaurants, art galleries, meeting areas, hostelries and a bocce ball court.

HUNTER MUSEUM

When Benjamin Franklin Thomas, one of the entrepreneurs who created Chattanooga's Coca-Cola bottling empire, decided to build a summer home on Lookout Mountain, his wife, Anne, looked at the majestic view and then at the frighteningly steep lot. "Well," she said, "Ben would."

Their nephew, George Thomas Hunter, later joined Anne Thomas to create a philanthropic organization in Thomas's memory. Named, aptly, the Benwood Foundation, its mission was "to promote religious, charitable, scientific, literary and educational activities for the advancement or well-being of mankind."

The centerpiece of the Benwood Foundation's gifts to our community is the majestic, classically southern building at 10 Bluff View that we now know as the Hunter Museum of American Art. In the 1920s, several years after her husband's death, Anne Thomas bought the graceful mansion on the river bluffs—inspired, no doubt, by yet another majestic view. Originally known as the Ross Faxon House, the mansion was designed by a Chicago architect, the son of a young man who was stationed in Chattanooga as a soldier in the Confederate army. Abram Garfield, the architect, was the son of President James A. Garfield, a man who learned courage on the battlefields of the Chattanooga valley.

Originally built by the Faxon family, this iconic building is home now to the Hunter Museum of American Art, a renowned collection housed in the mansion on the bluff.

It's easy to imagine that Indian scouts camped on those very bluffs, watching for the enemy and, possibly, seeking the same kind of inspiration in the beauty that Anne Thomas found there. Surely, during the Civil War, soldiers must have found the cliffs over the winding Tennessee River a strategic lookout, and they may have found some solace in the beauty of the view.

While the Bluff View mansion may be the most striking gift the Benwood Foundation gave to Chattanooga, the foundation has helped enhance the quality of life in Chattanooga in countless ways. But it took a court battle to make it happen.

The Case for Art

When George Thomas Hunter died in 1950, some 70 percent of his estate was endowed to the Benwood Foundation. Tax laws, however, threatened to take millions away from the foundation and the many charities it would benefit. The family fought in a precedent-setting lawsuit; a 1952 ruling for the Benwood Foundation became case law regarding charitable donations.

Can you imagine spending money to make sure that your relative's money was given away according to his wishes? Well, that is a part of the deep generosity and family spirit that are as vibrant here as the natural beauty.

The View: Food for the Spirit

Maybe the Scenic City brings out the best in its citizens; after all, there is something about a beautiful view that can make your spirit soar. It can inspire you to be better, do better and dream better.

The view is especially lovely when you see it reflected in children's eyes. As a parent, it thrills me to take my boys to a special little side road where the view of the bridges, the magnificent cliffs and the Hunter Museum soars in front of us. Rising above that panorama is the sometimes clouded vista of Lookout Mountain, and below is the ever-flowing ribbon that is the Tennessee River.

There is awe in the eyes of children when they drink in that view and own it as their history, community and future. Walking through the Hunter Museum, they have that same look of wonder, their senses surging as they absorb and are inspired by the art that's part of their own world.

Imagine if it were not that way, if there were no art in Chattanooga, no community revitalization, no extra funding for schools—all products of the vision of families committed to our city, its families and art.

Doing as "Ben Would"

When members of the Benwood Foundation realized that nine of the twenty lowest-performing schools in Tennessee were in Chattanooga, they responded with an act of philanthropy in the spirit of their historic benefactors, Benjamin Thomas and his nephew, George Thomas Hunter. The Benwood Foundation endowed the local Public Education Foundation with a $5 million grant designed to raise student achievement.

That 2001 initiative is a part of a larger network of philanthropic alliances that the Public Education Foundation's Dan Challener calls "a catalyst for dramatic improvement." David Carroll, reporter for WRCB-TV Channel 3, beams when he talks about the "boosted test scores and improved teacher retention" seen in the system since the initiative began, and the Terra Nova Achievement tests that continue to reflect consistent improvement.

Now, sixteen Hamilton County schools and the families they serve are reaping the reward of the dreams of George Hunter and his aunt, Anne Thomas—who knew that "Ben would."

The Bluff View Arts District is now home to museums, sculpture gardens and eateries that celebrate the beauty of a district that was once home to mansions and millionaires.

Art, New Life at Bluff View

With the Hunter Museum as its focal point, the Bluff View Arts District has been freshly imbued with the spirit of art and life. Since the early 1990s, Dr. Charles and Mary Portera have worked to combine art, public art, food and family to create an arts district that tantalizes all of the senses.

Now the Bluff View is a perfect place to make family memories, from a game of bocce ball to a stroll through the sculpture garden. If art is life and life is art, family is at the middle of it all—and it's alive and well in the Bluff View and in Chattanooga's vibrant arts community.

HOUSTON MUSEUM

Whether she married nine men or ten, what isn't disputed is that during her colorful life, "Antique Annie" amassed what is considered the finest collection of glass and ceramics in the world. Her "pretties," now housed in

The Houston Museum is one of the great jewels of the district, home to the largest collection of glassware of its kind in the world, the collection a gift to the children of Chattanooga.

a Victorian house in the Bluff View Arts District, are but a fraction of what was a massive collection, handpicked by a self-taught master in the art of discovering, recognizing and acquiring antiques of all kinds.

Born in 1876 in Evening Shade, Arkansas, Anna Safley had to quit school in the sixth grade to care for her nine younger siblings when their mother and newborn brother died. In a life characterized by energy and determination, such personal losses punctuated the spirit of success but never dimmed her resolve. A courageous young girl, Anna was a rare breed when she struck out on her own to seek her fortune. Imagine a fifteen-year-old girl traveling alone from Arkansas to Chicago, bankrolled by money she had earned teaching children barely older than herself!

That journey lasted a lifetime. In her search for beautiful things, Anna traveled to every state in the Union, toured Canada and even dodged the bullets of Pancho Villa to buy antiques in war-torn Mexico. No one knows exactly how she managed to fund her valuable acquisitions, which over time grew to the tens of thousands.

She also collected suitors, marrying at least nine times (or more, according to some rumors), with her second marriage bringing her to Chattanooga.

Anna Safley Houston was a strong businesswoman, unique character and remarkable collector, her amazing gift to Chattanooga representing her life's work.

But the woman who collected property, husbands, antiques and art cared more for their legacy than for herself or her health. Her only offspring—two daughters from her first marriage—died in infancy, and reports varied about her feelings on children. She often sat, cold and hungry, in a warehouse full of priceless antiques she refused to sell. And while her later years were characterized by poverty, eccentricity and harrowing escapes from fire, thieves and creditors, her passion for the future of her collection remained steadfast.

The Name that Stayed

Over the course of her many marriages, several of the divorce proceedings reported incidents of physical abuse, and others described men intent on being supported by this strong woman. But none of those men was able to deter Anna from the goal that was the beacon of her life—to turn her collection into a museum.

Anna Safley changed her name often, reverting to her family name as each marriage ended. The exception was her eighth marriage, to plumber and handyman James Houston, who remained her friend and correspondent until her death. When her final marriage ended, it was his name to which she reverted and that she honored in her instructions for the museum housing her collection to bear the Houston name.

Zeal and Determination

Had the Depression not sunk her business, Anna Safley Houston could have been one of the strongest business owners in Chattanooga. Her hat store, antique shops and property rental business were all successful examples of her determination, skill and business acumen. At one time, she owned many of the buildings on McCallie Avenue and was landlord to many McCallie School students.

Mrs. Houston was known for her business acumen, her memory for detail, her fair dealings with banks and her leadership in the Chattanooga business community. Though her appearance and comfort were secondary concerns to her, it was a well turned-out lady whom neighbors saw boarding trains, bound for buying trips—barely recognizable from the poor, dowdy, dirty woman they would later call "Antique Annie."

In her later years, Mrs. Houston was known for her reluctance to pay bills and for the squalor and poor conditions in which she lived. At age sixty, still attractive to men decades younger, she single-handedly built a ramshackle warehouse for "her pretties" in what is now East Ridge. Neighbors would see her walking to the railroad depot to collect the heavy packages that arrived COD; often she would manage heavy loads by moving them down the street half at a time, always pushing steadily toward her goal.

She pursued the goal of her museum and the acquisition of items for its teaching mission with the same determination. Passion and single-mindedness guided her steps as she carried heavy loads, hobo-style, on her frequent fifteen-mile journeys with her treasures.

"Antique Annie"

Customer service was not a part of the older Annie's style. Though she ran a warehouse store, she not only screened people before allowing them in but also unceremoniously removed offensive customers without explanation, whether they were rich or not.

She would sell an item only to help pay for a higher-quality piece but was known to give tiny pieces, often chipped, to children in the hopes of inspiring them to appreciate antique art. And when she died, she bequeathed her entire beloved collection to her adopted hometown.

Sharing her treasures and their history with the children of Chattanooga was a dream that motivated Anna Safley Houston through most of her life, and her collection, fabled for its amazing worth, is testament to the determination of a woman with a goal. That dream did not become reality until nearly a decade after her death in 1951, but now the Houston Museum is a regular Mecca, drawing people from around the world to rooms that dance with light reflected from one of the finest glass collections in the world.

RUTH HOLMBERG GLASS BRIDGE

The crystal clear connection that guides guests from the Hunter Museum toward the revitalized riverfront community of the Walnut Street Bridge, the Tennessee Aquarium and Ross's Landing is a metaphor for the bridges that Ruth and Bill Holmberg built in their community.

The Holmberg Pedestrian Bridge celebrates the memory of Bill Holmberg. As a civic leader and *Chattanooga Times* executive, Bill Holmberg and his wife, Ruth, the granddaughter of Adolph Ochs, served his spirit by providing their city and its people with clear news and a connection to the arts.

Enthusiastic supporters of the arts, the imprint of the Holmberg's philanthropy can be seen in the sights, sounds and scenes of Chattanooga's art community and the associations that support it.

TENNESSEE AQUARIUM

The Tennessee Aquarium follows a raindrop from an Appalachian forest to the Gulf, telling its story from the mountains to the sea. Freshwater and saltwater habitats connect the Tennessee River to the Gulf and its visitors to their own natural world.

Glass peaks, the winged art of birds and butterflies and the underwater majesty of fresh- and saltwater life inspire guests to embrace the diverse and dynamic world under the waters of our global and local community.

Built in 1992 as part of Jack T. Lupton's dream for the revitalization of the Scenic City, the idea of the Tennessee Aquarium began in a 1984 community visioning process that would shape the way that Chattanoogans approached change. Chattanooga Venture began in the chamber of commerce, was buoyed by the Lyndhurst Foundation and found its legs in the dynamic change that the team saw made in Indianapolis. The Vision 2000 process capitalized on the enthusiasm for change, and the fervor spread as Chattanooga's charm grew.

Working together to promote meaningful development, public access, enrichment and enjoyment, the Moccasin Bend Task Force and Chattanooga citizens launched a renaissance that would forever change Chattanooga. Embracing the past and celebrating the present, public and private partnerships worked together to open the Chattanooga Area Visitors' Center (1993), the Creative Discovery Museum (1995), the IMAX 3-D (1996), the Walnut Street Pedestrian Bridge (1993) and Coolidge Park (1999).

These efforts catapulted Chattanooga into the national limelight as the city began to be celebrated nationwide for its clean environment, natural beauty and high quality of life.

COCA-COLA BOTTLING

J.T. Lupton, one of the three original Coca-Cola bottling partners, created a family spirit of philanthropy that led to the Lyndhurst Foundation and other efforts to revitalize Chattanooga.

Young and adventurous, three transplants to Chattanooga bought the bottling rights for Coca-Cola for one dollar, and in 1899, one of the most well-branded items in the world took life in Chattanooga. The iconic bottle and effervescent drink earned a place in the hearts of Americans at home and abroad, as the company supplied soldiers in World Wars and the franchise spread across the country. Designed in 1929 by local architect William Crutchfield, the Broad Street bottling plant was built on the original site of the Chattanooga Brewery and could produce up to 144,000 bottles each day.

The legacy of the company continued to be felt in the downtown

B.F. Thomas, J.B. Whitehead and J.T. Lupton were the original Coca-Cola bottling partners. The legacy of their efforts and philanthropy has been changing Chattanooga since 1899.

area even after the Broad Street plant was sold to Royal Crown Bottling. The Lyndhurst Foundation, created by the family of J.T. Lupton, directed much of the change that heralded Chattanooga as a city celebrated for its environmental change, quality of life and natural beauty.

SOUTHERN BELLE

Chattanooga boasts approximately nine thousand hotel rooms that maintain an average of 75 percent occupancy. The draw of the Scenic City is more than the inspiring mountains, majestic under-the-earth experiences and unforgettable vistas. The South is a culture of civility, gentility and charm as thick as the scent of magnolia blossoms that can hang in the humid air.

American families have been following the Chapin family's "See Rock City" barns toward the Scenic City, attracted by the lure of the idolized

South but drawn back by the natural beauty and unique cultural identity of a city with heritage that runs deeper than just one culture, era or time period.

The *Southern Belle* is a five-hundred-passenger riverboat that has lunch and dinner cruises embracing the gentility of the South with the sounds, sights and flavors that keep families coming back to the Scenic City.

SUNKEN HISTORY

Several sunken sites lie under the waters of the Tennessee River. The *Tellico* was a steamer that had been converted to a ferry and sank in 1886, joined in the murky depths by the Chattanooga riverboat that capsized and sank in 1920. Each year, local divers and environmental advocates work to clear the river's bottom of debris, exploring these wrecks and the federal pontoon boats farther downstream.

CAMERON HILL

Raw, scraped earth colors the western horizon overlooking downtown Chattanooga. Dirt makes a brown line, erasing the grass, trees and homes where people lived, loved and were Chattanoogans.

That's the scene today as you drive on Highway 27 toward Signal Mountain. And it was the scene in the early 1950s, when a group of citizens led by a few striking and strident women lost a battle to save houses, neighborhoods and, yes, 150 feet of a mountain with a shape and point resembling its larger neighbor, Lookout.

Painting Pays a Pinnacle

When James Cameron, a famous nineteenth-century artist, painted a historical portrait of Chattanooga's Whiteside family in the 1850s, he was paid what may still be a record purchase price for a portrait. Colonel James Whiteside, a state senator, gave Cameron prime real estate overlooking Chattanooga's downtown. Area residents soon began calling it Cameron Hill.

In June 1862, this small mountain was the site of the first Civil War engagement in Chattanooga, a city known by Abraham Lincoln and other leaders to be "the most important place in the whole war field…its capture would mean the end of the war" as described in John Wilson's

This postcard shows the Walnut and Market Street Bridges with Cameron Hill and Lookout Mountain in the background, their similar profiles still intact.

book, *Chattanooga's Story.* Besieged on Cameron Hill, the Union army used every tree and root available for heat and construction of its breastworks and military machinery. Even the centuries-old trees that had covered the mountain were felled.

After the ravages of war, Cameron Hill was nothing but bare earth. In an unsung and unreimbursed effort, a lone city councilman, Isaac Mansfield, replanted the barren hill. Mrs. Cameron, who had fled during the war to California, sued the government for reimbursement of the trees and eventually won an astounding compensation of $30,000.

Cameron Casino—and a Council in a Cave

By the end of the nineteenth century, pre–Civil War homes were joined by stately homes as the city's elite were attracted to the pinnacle rising abruptly from downtown with majestic views of Missionary Ridge, Lookout Mountain, Signal Mountain and Stringer's Ridge. During its heyday, Cameron Hill was home to a casino resort and, in 1889, Chattanooga's first incline railway, a 1,500-foot track up the mountainside.

While Cameron Hill remained a premier neighborhood well into the mid-twentieth century, the casino was not very popular, and both it and the incline lasted only a few years. But in the course of business the casino manager did make a remarkable discovery close to the resort site: a cave housing skeletal evidence of what may have been an early Chattanooga "council" meeting.

In 1957, Richard Palmer of the *News Free Press* wrote that the casino manager discovered the cave with what appeared to be the remains of Native American chiefs and near-chiefs. Zella Armstrong, longtime Hamilton County historian, reported several times that her sources claimed that "the bodies were in sitting position and that a score (20) or more were present."

Freeway Fracas

In November 1955, Chattanooga mayor P.R. Olgiati made an announcement that aroused the ire of many citizens and stirred a group of staunch preservationists to outright anger. The national freeway system was a new idea; it was changing the landscape of the country and significantly impacting the economic development of many cities. But Chattanooga's hills and mountains had prevented its inclusion in the original national plan, so the mayor and city council proposed an idea to bring the freeway and its benefits to Chattanooga.

Cameron Hill, officially a mountain, rose above downtown at 974 feet above mean sea level. If Cameron Hill were lowered to 817 feet, Olgiati said, the city could use the million cubic yards of fill dirt to raise the roadbed of the proposed freeway, and apartments could be built on the new, level hill.

Zella Armstrong was among the most vocal opponents of the plan. She was an influential citizen—not only county historian but also founder of the Cotton Ball and publisher of *The Lookout* magazine. She was one of a group of women who declared war on Olgiati's plans for the West Side.

Cameron Hill Crusaders

These "Cameron Hill Crusaders" fought valiantly. They were as concerned for the homes there—from mountaintop mansions like that of *New York Times* publisher Adolph Ochs to Bessie Smith's modest childhood home in Blue Goose Hollow at the foot of the mountain—as they were for the history and legacy of the land. Zella Armstrong recalled that when "Dr. Park McCallie said [in a public hearing] that he was 40 years old before he heard of Cameron Hill," she reminded the crowd that "his mother's brother was one of the defenders of the hill in that [Civil War] battle."

Eventually, the crusaders lost their battle to save the mountain they loved. The freeway was built, as were the apartments, which were razed to be replaced by BlueCross BlueShield's new, state-of-the-art headquarters, one of the largest building projects in Chattanooga's history.

But though Cameron Hill's shape has changed, its history has not. Today, while we watch the machinery again spread the red Tennessee clay, we should remember that history, from the council of chiefs in their long-gone cave and the Civil War soldiers who fought there to the Chattanooga women who so energetically defended the history and beauty of their beloved hometown.

BELLSOUTH PARK

The new home to the Chattanooga Lookouts looms above the streets that border Ross's Landing and the former home of Kirkman High School. The crack of baseballs and the cheers of crowds now resonate from Hawk Hill, named for the former school's mascot. Bellsouth Park, built in 2000, lives up to the storied heritage of the Chattanooga team, drawing families and visitors to the hill early residents called Reservoir Hill for its strategic placement for a water pumping system and reservoir that supported the growing downtown community.

CRUTCHFIELD HOUSE

"Procession of Secession" Leads to Chattanooga

Blood boiled and tempers were raging when Jefferson Davis stopped by Chattanooga's Crutchfield House. It was the end of January 1861, and a procession of secession had begun among the southern states, increasing tensions in the Deep South.

The first blood of the Civil War is historically known to have been shed at Fort Sumter, near Charleston, South Carolina. Yet a book published in 1881 includes a description of a remarkable event that shakes accepted Civil War and Chattanooga history. The tale is one of a city divided, families separated by beliefs and brothers on both sides of the question of war.

Chattanooga at that time was a bustling town, the flow of people and commerce steady—even as the region prepared for impending war. Tennessee was the last state to secede from the Union, and Chattanooga, with its rivers and railroads, was a hub of activity in an area bursting with tension.

Built by Thomas Crutchfield, the Crutchfield House was the first hotel in the city. Now the site of the Read House, the Crutchfield House was across from the first railroad depot.

Thomas Crutchfield the elder had come to Chattanooga, became the first professional contractor in the state of Tennessee and, by 1839, began to purchase land here, eventually erecting the Cabins, Chattanooga's first hostelry, in the shadow of the current BlueCross BlueShield headquarters on Pine Street. Traveling with his father-in-law, Samuel Cleage, and his Revolutionary War rifle, Kill Devil, Crutchfield brought a family history of fine brick-making and a résumé of houses and government buildings constructed from Virginia to Tennessee; among the notable structures he built in Chattanooga were First Presbyterian Church and James Whiteside's mansion on Cameron Hill.

Thomas set a good example for his children; both he and his sons served their adopted city in elected positions before, during and after the Civil War. In 1847, the family built the Crutchfield House across from the city's new rail terminal, and it became a thriving center of the bustling city.

This drawing of the Crutchfield House depicts an iconic landmark since 1850, legendary for the duel that was almost fought there between William Crutchfield and Jefferson Davis.

Dilemma of a Duel Denied

The story of the duel that was almost fought between Jefferson Davis and Chattanooga's William Crutchfield spread like wildfire in the news-hungry papers in those days prior to the outbreak of war. It has been repeated for generations in Chattanooga lore and was the only reference to our city in Paul Johnson's 1999 tome, *History of the American People.*

The story goes that Jefferson Davis was rushing to Mississippi after having resigned his Senate seat, hurrying to his expected election as president of the newly forming Confederate States of America. Drawn inexorably to Chattanooga, the funnel of the world, he stopped at the Crutchfield House for respite and was called by citizens to address an assembled crowd.

Retiring after his comments, Davis was swept up in a furor as word came that the Unionist William Crutchfield had denounced him as a traitor. In a fiery speech atop a table, fist brandished, Crutchfield labeled Davis a "future military despot," refuting Davis's call to secede. The story accepted as legend holds that his brother, Thomas Crutchfield, a Southern sympathizer himself, pulled William off the table—and thus narrowly averted the duel that could have changed the course of the Civil War.

First Blood Makes New History?

Louis Jarrell Dupre, known in print as "the Newspaper Man," was both a college-educated journalist and a law school graduate. His career included

John Crawford Vaughn, who later became a sheriff in Monroe County, was traveling with Jefferson Davis to Mississippi when Davis became embroiled in debate at the Crutchfield House.

extensive newspaper work before the Civil War, postwar service to President Grover Cleveland and years of experience as a Confederate army scout, from which he based a book published in 1881.

In a chapter entitled "First Blood Spilled," Dupre reported that during the encounter made legendary at the Crutchfield House, a man named John Vaughn defended Davis's honor and broke a black bottle over the head of Bill Crutchfield, who was then "borne helpless and senseless from the scene of the conflict, shedding the first blood spilled in the war."

Could this be true? Can there be any new discoveries in the history of a war we thought we knew? In fact, history can be as exciting as the unknown future as long as modern-day investigators—historians, archivists, students, even hobbyists—work to uncover new dimensions of long-held stories. Louis Dupre's historic reference may have remained unknown had the University of North Carolina not embarked upon a program to digitalize documents from early southern history.

Internet research reveals logs and records verifying that there was, indeed, a Civil War soldier named John Crawford Vaughn who accompanied Jefferson Davis as he left the Senate for Mississippi. Vaughn was made a brigadier general during the Civil War and was one of the five brigade commanders who took part in the last council of war held by President Davis in Abbeville, South Carolina, and led the escort guarding Davis at the close of the war.

History with Us

Descendants of some key players in this story are still prominent in Chattanooga today. After the Civil War, members of the Crutchfield family continued to lead the city. William Crutchfield became a congressman, Thomas Crutchfield was a mayor and brought agricultural advances to the area and together the brothers helped establish the First National Bank at the close of the war. Nearly 150 years after the fiery Unionist's tabletop speech, a new generation of Crutchfields—William, Ward and Tom—are all attorneys practicing in Chattanooga, and many buildings still bear the mark of the current William's father, the architect William Crutchfield.

William Crutchfield, son of early Chattanooga developer Thomas Crutchfield, decried Jefferson Davis as a future military despot.

And the Crutchfield House? During the Civil War it was the first building in Chattanooga to be occupied by Union the ground in 1867. Four years later, a doctor named John Read built a new hotel on the site. During the boom of the 1917 period, businesses like a roller coaster with bench seats and a Turkish bath drew residents and tourists to the area. The Read House, since then rebuilt and renovated, stands at the corner of Broad and Ninth Streets—a stately reminder of the duel that almost was and an iconic building that recalls the history of the city in portraits, the gracious spirit of service and the occasional ghostly visit of its southern spirits.

CHATTANOOGA–HAMILTON COUNTY BICENTENNIAL LIBRARY

A two-dollar-per-citizen donation from Andrew Carnegie supported the creation of the Chattanooga Public Library at the corner of Georgia Avenue in 1905. The Carnegie Library was at the site of the First District School, established in 1880 and moved to a new facility on Market Street in 1976. The Chattanooga–Hamilton County Bicentennial Library remains the stalwart headquarters of the library system. Programs and outreach support Chattanoogans of all ages with a remarkable Regional History Department, active Children's Section and impressive online resources. The Chattanooga–Hamilton County Bicentennial Library is supported by the City of Chattanooga and the Friends of the Library, which host an innovative yearly event to augment the programs and services offered.

SINGLE STEEPLE

Since 1882, a majestic stone steeple has inspired Chattanoogans to reach toward the heavens, a beacon of light and hope for the generations who struggled to rebuild a city ravaged by the Civil War. "The Old Stone Church" at the corner of McCallie and Georgia Avenues, which served a congregation organized in 1865, brought dignity, spirituality and hope to one of the busiest corners of a bustling Chattanooga.

Today's Chattanoogans drive by, their eyes following the spire up toward the sky, only to realize as they pass that the beautiful, patina-streaked steeple is the cornerstone of a parking lot, not a place of worship.

How did this beautiful landmark become a place for cars instead of souls, and what secrets does it hold about our city's history?

From Ross's Landing to the Mountain

Chattanooga Welcomes "Transplants"

Many have theorized that Chattanooga should have become the enormous city that Atlanta is. (It's whispered that the "powers that be" kept Chattanooga to a modest size based on their personal whims.) Geographically, Chattanooga has been the crossroads of the South since buffalo blazed trails that Native Americans, pioneers, railroads and highways would follow. Those trails were complemented by a river system that encouraged travel and commerce.

Local businessman Jack McDonald, whose family started the Peerless Woolen Mills, credits the political climate of the post–Civil War era for the differences between the reconstruction of Chattanooga and Atlanta. When the call came to rebuild broken cities, he says, Atlanta was a less friendly environment than Chattanooga, which welcomed entrepreneurs from both sides of the war who shared the vision of a New South.

In 1882, there were already seventy-seven manufacturing plants here, businesses owned by both native Chattanoogans and those who came here to join in the rebirth of the city. By 1885, when that landmark stone church and steeple were built, Chattanooga boasted a robust population of twenty-five thousand. Many of its staunchest citizens originally came here from the North, fell in love with the city—and stayed.

North/South Split

In the 1800s, the national Methodist Church mirrored the nation, split into North and South. The southern denomination, which after several name changes became Centenary Methodist, would serve the religious needs of families whose names still resonate in Chattanooga today, including the Warners, the Cravenses and the Crutchfields.

In 1865, a minister from Ohio serving Union soldiers billeted in Chattanooga organized a "northern" First Methodist Episcopal Church here. The congregation of soldiers and citizens was small but devout; that group of sixteen people would grow into a church with missionaries all over the world. It served the poor in Chattanooga, built a Methodist college (1886) that evolved into the University of Tennessee at Chattanooga and was home to the first resident bishop in Tennessee, a descendant of Elijah Walden, for whom our Walden's Ridge is named.

Where the Hamilton County Courthouse now stands, First Methodist shared a space with a Baptist congregation. In 1885, they built their own church at the corner of McCallie and Georgia. That year a *Chattanooga Times* article described the structure as the "embodiment of grace in architecture." The stones, mined from the Beck quarry on the property that is now the Chattanooga Golf and Country Club, came together to make a "lofty spire which clefts the clouds, a beacon for miles and miles, directing the thoughts of the beholder to the heaven to which it points." Stalwart citizens like the Whelands, Pattens, Fergers, Dyers and Wilders would find their spiritual home in that "Old Stone Church."

Churches Merge

In 1939, the northern and southern branches of the national Methodist Church combined. Nearly three decades later, the two local churches followed suit, merging in 1967 to form First-Centenary United Methodist.

Chattanoogans were celebrating the Sabbath in this church when the Union cannons began their onslaught from Stringer's Ridge. The spire was a beacon of hope for generations of Chattanoogans.

The two congregations—which would have been considered enemies during wartime—together erected a new place of worship on the site of what had been Centenary Methodist on McCallie Avenue. The congregants loved Chattanooga enough to make it a place to live safely and happily and to raise children who would work together for a better future.

When the new church was built, the Street family ensured that each building that had housed the congregants of this combined ministry was represented in its design; in appreciation for both congregations, the Streets donated the inspiring stained-glass windows that still color the sun as it meets the sanctuary. (The Streets are another family with roots in the Stone Church; the current Gordon Street's great-grandfather was a Union soldier who served picket duty on Stringer's Ridge and who, after working in mining, moved his sons to Chattanooga, a place that had captured his heart.)

Saving a Spire

The grace of that church's congregation still illuminates our city. The impact of the Street family can be seen in the revitalization of the Dome Building, the Stone Church and other projects and people that have made much of Chattanooga what it is today. Gordon Street's great-uncle was William Brock Sr., whose grandsons would include presidents of Covenant College and Brock Candy and a United States senator. Through acts of faith, these families helped shape the landscape of Chattanooga, and it was faith that inspired the Streets' business, North American Royalties, to work to save the steeple that has graced our downtown for so long.

After the two Methodist churches merged, the fate of the venerable Stone Church was in jeopardy; the building was no longer structurally sound. North American Royalties combined its practical need for parking with its desire to maintain the integrity of the historic skyline and designed a project that would serve both needs, saving the spire.

The descendant of that church, First-Centenary, continues to grow. Church member Mai Bell Hurley has worked both as a city council member and as a community volunteer to improve Chattanooga. When she talks about projects at First-Centenary and its surrounding neighborhood, her eyes glow with the same passion that motivated the women of the Stone Church, who 125 years ago raised money coin by coin and cake by cake to build that beautiful steeple.

Meanwhile, First-Centenary United Methodist Church and its McCallie Avenue neighborhood are bustling with construction and congeniality.

Congregants are working together to further the goals of their city and their ever-growing ministry, a perfect celebration of the spirit that made Chattanooga and its churches thrive into what we enjoy today.

THOMAS MCCALLIE HOUSE

An early mercantile store and family home occupied the land at the corner of McCallie Avenue and Lindsay Street, built shortly after the 1841 arrival of Thomas McCallie and his family. The twenty-five-acre farm was a popular stopping point on the road between Ross's Landing and the Brainerd Mission, eventually earning the road the name McCallie Avenue in celebration of the family who anchored the area.

Occupied during much of the Civil War by Union soldiers, this family property would later serve as the site of the first Baylor School in 1893.

GOLDEN DOME BUILDING

Is it gold that glitters on the dome downtown? Since 1892, the sun has sparkled around Georgia Avenue's Dome Building, our city's first "skyscraper," and the spirit behind its creation and renovation could only be found in Chattanooga.

That gold-domed cupola is striking, and its history is fascinating, centered on a man whose life and career impacted journalism and the modern world. Though born in Ohio, Adolph Ochs called Chattanooga home, and the city's place in his heart was clear throughout his life and career.

A House Divided, but Together

Imagine parenting six children during the tumult of the Civil War and its aftermath. Now imagine the added burden that comes from being "different." As Jewish immigrants from Bavaria, Julius and Bertha Ochs shared a different heritage than most Chattanoogans. And as husband and wife, they were different from each other, holding opposite beliefs about the war raging around them.

Bertha was a firebrand who believed deeply, strongly and with a passion that emboldened her to carry her infant, Adolph, across enemy lines, smuggling quinine to wounded Confederate soldiers. Julius, who upon immigration to

The Dome Building, built by Adoph Ochs, was a beacon for Chattanoogans, its golden dome symbolizing hope for a struggling city.

the United States had enthusiastically embraced his adopted country, served as a Union soldier. He was a tolerant, quiet and steadfast parent, fluent in six languages and well versed in the classics, mathematics and military strategy. He demanded honesty, financial integrity and courage, and he modeled these qualities as a father, husband, soldier and business owner.

It's no surprise that these forceful people raised a son who set the international standard for objective, courageous and responsible journalism. Raised in postwar Knoxville and a wage earner since the age of eleven, as a teenager Adolph moved to Chattanooga to take a job at the *Chattanooga Dispatch*. When that newspaper hit hard times, nineteen-year-old Adolph found himself without a job in a city he'd fallen in love with. So he took a leap of faith: he borrowed $250 and bought the *Dispatch*'s competition, which he renamed the *Chattanooga Times*. The principles he learned from his parents enabled Adolph to produce a paper that was "clean, dignified and trustworthy."

In 1884, Adolph married Effie Wise. Though they lost several children to miscarriages and stillbirths, they did have one daughter, Iphigenia, who later would stand at the helm of a titanic newspaper empire.

A Sign of Faith in Changing Chattanooga

Embraced by his new city, Adolph Ochs devoted his tireless energy to rebuilding Chattanooga, a city that had been on the front lines of the Civil War. He was instrumental in the first reunion event at the Chickamauga battlefield, which had soaked up the blood of men from both sides of the war. His influence was behind many pivotal changes in postwar Chattanooga. But in 1887, the economy of the South began to fail. The development boom that Adolph Ochs had helped cultivate began to crash around Chattanooga and the enterprises of its adopted son.

The *Chattanooga Times* was an Ochs family operation; most of the family lived together in a stately home on Cameron Hill. They had long dreamed of relocating the newspaper offices, and in 1892, construction of the *Times* building was finished. While fortunes were crumbling around the city, a *Chattanooga Times* article recalls that the "building was for some months at that time the only conspicuous indication of local confidence of Chattanooga's ability to pass through the depression so prevalent throughout the south."

Some ten thousand people are reported to have attended the grand opening of this fine building. Later, when at this same building the city honored Adolph Ochs, the luminaries shone brighter than even the dome as they celebrated the man who had been so important in changing the future of a southern city.

The Man with the Golden Touch

While the dome and the *Chattanooga Times* it housed remained integral to the city, Ochs threw his lucky dice one more time and, armed with $70,000 and a letter from President Grover Cleveland, purchased the *New York Times*. A man with the golden touch, he began the tradition of Times Square pyrotechnics when he included a street-level fireworks show in a 1904 New Year's Eve party celebrating the opening of his new building at 1 Times Square.

From Ross's Landing to the Mountain

Built by Adolph Ochs, the golden top of the *Chattanooga Times* headquarters was one of the city's first skyscrapers, its construction heralding hope during a time of depression.

The man who built a golden dome to support the future of a city he loved parlayed his commitment to fair journalism and belief in himself into an empire, which continues to rule at the *New York Times*. After his remarkable achievement at the *Times*, he never speculated in other businesses, seeming content to leave a family imbued with the values that his parents gave him.

Adolph Ochs was described in a flamboyant era as a boring family man; he was always willing to listen to the concerns or questions of his employees, family and friends. But he was also a man consulted by presidents, a remarkable icon influenced by the spirit that was alive in Chattanooga. Ochs's commitment to our city continues to resonate through the works of his granddaughter, Ruth Holmberg, who became publisher of the *Chattanooga Times Free Press*.

The dome that once marked the old *Times* building may not be made of solid gold, but the impact of Adolph Ochs continues to glow, spreading across Chattanooga from that beautiful building on Georgia Avenue.

FOUNTAIN SQUARE

Chattanooga was made Hamilton County's county seat in 1870, its original county seat now resting under the waters of the Chickamauga Lake. The county courthouse became the center of the political city, and when a tragic Market Street fire claimed the lives of two brave firefighters, their sacrifice was commemorated in an 1888 fountain built across from the courthouse. The three-tiered fountain was added to the Registry of Historic Places in 1979 and was once the center of a pen that held alligators, a draw for curious spectators but a danger for residents, as escaped alligators roamed the streets.

SOLOMON FEDERAL BUILDING

In a city known for its panoramic views, one of the most spectacular is the view from the courtroom of the Joel W. Solomon Federal Building. The view is not out the window but on the wall above the judge's bench in a third-floor

The Solomon Building was part of the New Deal era. Built by the iconic architect R.H. Hunt, this building is known for its lines, beauty and for hosting the jury-tampering trial of Jimmy Hoffa.

courtroom, where a curving mural—seventeen feet long and five feet tall—depicts a visual allegory of our city's history. The courtroom is the most historically significant room in one of Chattanooga's most architecturally important buildings, sitting at the heart of the city.

The room itself is inspiring, its gleaming, inlaid wood and majestic furniture providing a warm contrast to the building's cool, marble hallways. While the corridors of the Solomon Building have echoed with the historic footsteps of controversial figures like union leader Jimmy Hoffa and anti-TVA activist Jo Conn Guild, the building's art and design were inspired and created by leaders like Franklin Delano Roosevelt and iconic regional architect R.H. Hunt.

FDR's Public Art

What we now call the Solomon Building was constructed from 1932 to 1933 as the U.S. Post Office and Courthouse, and the mural was installed in 1937, the result of a public art program that was part of FDR's New Deal. The Treasury Department's Section of Painting and Sculpture operated both to serve Depression-era communities and to provide talented artists with gainful employment. "The Section" commissioned sculptures and murals in post offices in over 1,100 cities, including thirty works in post offices in Tennessee.

The Treasury Department's Procurement Division, which administered the program, was led by lawyer, businessman and artist Edward Bruce. Bruce was charged with selecting art of high quality to decorate public buildings.

The Section provided that 1 percent of a federal building's funding went to "embellishments" and ensured that the commissioned murals honored each city and were designed in partnership with the community. The result was a truly democratic art form. The artworks' presence in post offices—hubs of citizenry—meant that they were genuinely accessible to the public.

In Chattanooga, the Section's efforts were manifest in two works: a metal sculpture of a postman and a mural depicting the city's history, both still on display in the courthouse building.

The Architect and the Artist

That building was constructed for $493,000 and designed by R.H. Hunt, a prodigious architect whose five decades of work changed the landscape of Chattanooga. Hunt designed every major public building constructed in Chattanooga between 1895 and 1935, as well as landmark buildings like

Second Presbyterian Church and the St. John's Hotel. For the U.S. Post Office and Courthouse, his last major work, Hunt collaborated with the New York designers of the Empire State Building.

In 1938, the courthouse won the American Institute of Architects award as one of the 150 finest buildings constructed in the previous two decades. It was later voted into the National Register of Historic Places as part of a thematic group of buildings designed by the legendary man.

Hunt was part of the five-person local committee who worked with the Section and the artist chosen for the mural, a young watercolorist named Hilton Leech.

A City, Illustrated

Allegory of Chattanooga, Leech's panorama, mesmerizes as the viewer's eye sweeps past painted figures so fine that each could be a significant portrait. His representation of Chattanooga's history is designed to reinforce the New Deal message of optimism, hard work and revolutionary technology.

Viewed in concert, the images conjure a feeling of movement while telling the story of a land and its people. The federal government and the local committee examined and approved each image, intended to convey local pride while tying city history to the federal courtroom.

The faces in the mural are those of soldiers, nurses, Cherokee, pioneers, railway workers, a slave, a pastor and a frontiersman. They seem to move in time and place among familiar scenes (a dam, sprouting tobacco, a mountain range, a blue sky, a rustic cabin) and everyday objects (a train, a musket, a rifle, a cross, a blueprint, a Bible, bags of cotton and vegetables). Each person, place and thing represents some part of the city over whose justice the mural seems to preside.

Familiar Faces

To Chattanoogans, it's hard not to see in Leech's mural pastor Samuel Worcester, missionary to the Cherokees. Worcester took to the Supreme Court his fight to serve his flock—eventually following his beliefs all the way to a lonely jail cell, as President Andrew Jackson defied the court's order and began paving the Trail of Tears.

The TVA dam is clearly represented, but in the engineer with blueprints and younger assistant we might see Chattanooga's Guild family, engineers and entrepreneurs who built the first dam on the main channel of the

Tennessee River. These innovators took to the Supreme Court their case questioning the constitutionality of TVA and its eminent domain claim over their business assets. They brought hydroelectric power to the Chattanooga, Nashville and Knoxville markets as early as 1912, serving over 100,000 customers in over four hundred markets before losing their case in 1939.

In the Indians we might recognize the Cherokee at the Brainerd Mission, Ross's Landing or the Trail of Tears. The train could depict the railroads that turned Chattanooga into a center of commerce, while the railway worker might represent the tireless teams of men who picked and axed their way through Missionary Ridge and Tunnel Hill, giving the railroads access to Chattanooga's river traffic. That painted train could remind us of Andrews's Raiders, Union spies who screamed toward Chattanooga on a hijacked train, burning the rails behind them, bent on crippling the Confederacy by closing Chattanooga and the supply pipeline it represented.

The dead soldiers and the cross, labeled "1863," might represent any of the critical battles that took place in Chattanooga, while the rifle and musket stand for Revolutionary and Civil War battles and soldiers.

Healing, Reciprocated

Years before his inauguration, FDR became enamored of the landscape and people of this area as he sought healing from the chalybeate springs that flow naturally here. As president, he created New Deal programs to bring healing to this area and to a struggling nation.

The Solomon Building, erected under FDR's watch, stands as a testament of the interrelationship between U.S. government and its people. That building's centerpiece, *Allegory of Chattanooga*, illustrates the government's service to people—and the vital role those people play in their own communities.

CADEK

Chance, finance and happenstance met in a talented young man in 1892 and a gig at a place called Lookout Mountain. That meeting would forever change the destiny of the arts in Chattanooga. His nostrils still stung with brine from the sea voyage when Joseph O. Cadek joined his troupe for a railroad trip to the Lookout Inn, atop Lookout Mountain in the Tennessee Valley.

The Cadek Conservatory is part of the University of Tennessee at Chattanooga, its founding reflecting the cultural wealth that European immigrants brought to early Chattanooga.

Joseph spoke no English when he traveled from Prague to Boston, the musical center of the United States. He was a violin virtuoso and a hot commodity in the musical world, and he finally chose to live in Chattanooga and brought his Parisian-born fiancée here to start their family.

Their four children they would have were born in the valleys that reminded him of his early years but as the founding family of the artistic life of a city. Joseph's talent was extraordinary, and he was highly sought after, playing in the hotspots of turn-of-the-century America, recruiting artists to visit and teach students in his adopted city.

He played a solo in 1898 for President and Mrs. McKinley and the Supreme Court, with an equal fervor teaching Chattanooga children the theory and passion of the violin. He taught at Normal University, gave private lessons to children and worked to start the first musical societies of the city, professional gigs in larger cities likely funding his love of living in this valley.

The convenience of the railroad and the strength of Cadek's ability as a musical promoter and teacher led to a vibrant arts community in a newly revitalizing city. Heralded as the most important single influence on the growth of music in Chattanooga, the birth of the Cadek Conservatory came in 1904 and promised thorough instruction from beginning until finish.

The Birth of a School in the Heart of a Family

Classes began on January 1, 1905, and the first recital was on January 19, an amazing eighteen days later. The enthusiasm with which Dr. Cadek and his staff taught mesmerized Chattanooga and inspired pupils from six months old to octogenarians. The Cadek Conservatory has always been dedicated to training individuals in the fine arts and fostering musical awareness in the entire community.

The secret of the birth of the arts in Chattanooga is in the family, and the Cadek Conservatory was a family institution. The convergence of rail lines

A native of Prague, Joseph Cadek played at the White House for President William McKinley and settled in Chattanooga after working at the Lookout Inn in 1893.

in Chattanooga brought artists through town, many of whom, like Cadek, lived here as a base for their work travels. Having so many artists in residence benefited the arts community, choirs, choruses, theaters and the community that so embraced them.

He lauded his adopted city for its many concerts, extolling them because "what sets the city apart from all other cities of its size in the South is the variety and importance of the music that is produced by its own citizens."

The 1890 Census reported 29,100 residents in Chattanooga, people from twenty-seven states and eleven foreign countries. There were 283 business and 56 industries in the city, a community experiencing a marked economic growth despite a general national recession. The popularity of the nation's first National Battlefield Park and the railroad system began drawing tourists to the Scenic City, many of whom had served in an epic Civil War battle.

Housed in its earliest days in the former home of the Mizpah Congregation Synagogue on 241 Walnut Street and then moved to the University of Chattanooga campus, the sounds of the Cadek Conservatory were the same. In 1925, it was the largest school of its kind in the South, and in 1928, it was honored with a fellow from the Julliard Foundation in New York. The Cadek Conservatory made Chattanooga the musical center of the South, offering instruction in dancing, fine arts, dramatic arts, piano theory, wind instruments, voice, violin and viola and remaining consistently devoted to music for and by Chattanoogans.

Joseph and his bride died five years apart after lives lived well, and the legacy of their mutual loves for the family, arts and city remain as a gift to all Chattanoogans today. Families with names like Whiteside, Strang, Temple, Holtzclaw and Ferger traveled in pony buggies up Georgia Avenue to the Cadek Conservatory to hear the music of their children's voices, the parents returning for concerts to hear the world's most famous artists.

The Cadeks, both talented artists, loving parents and devout Chattanoogans, believed the early years were a magical time when children could learn amazing things. Their dedication to teaching children was one of the secrets in the strength and growth of the arts community of Chattanooga. Ottokar, Harold, Lillian and Theodora were the children of the Cadek couple, but they were reared alongside their other children: the opera, choral, symphony and chamber music organizations. Their spirit and family love of music also fostered choirs, youth musical groups and family musical gatherings that have offspring alive today.

Joseph Cadek was a virtuoso of the violin, a master of the musical theory, a teacher who inspired not just the student but also its family and a man who led a small school to honors and membership from Julliard, the National Association of the Schools of Music and the National Guild of Community Schools of the Arts. The Cadek Conservatory embraced students who were babies, learning with their families how to first control things by making sounds, a revolutionary idea in education embraced by a city eager to encourage arts in education and society.

More importantly, the thing that defined the man was his relationship with his wife and children. The man with a lovable disposition and keen sense of humor was at the same time a stern disciplinarian who could never get the hang of putting the family car in reverse but was always adept at moving Chattanooga's art community forward.

WALDEN HOSPITAL

In a time when equality between races was a goal too lofty to even be a dream, African Americans in Chattanooga were treated in the basements of local hospitals and even turned away from care in less tolerant communities.

Established by Dr. Emma Rochelle Wheeler, the Walden Hospital served the African American community for more than forty years and is a staid landmark in the now thriving UTC area.

Dr. Emma Rochelle Wheeler was a woman with powerful energy and commitment behind her oath to serve mankind. One of only three women in a graduating class of sixty-eight, Dr. Emma was already breaking new ground as a woman and as an African American when she and her husband chose to make their home in Chattanooga.

Both doctors, the Wheeler couple set out to serve the medical needs of Chattanooga's Negro community and in 1905 established a practice on East Main Street. After ten years there, Dr. Emma Wheeler established the Walden Hospital, erecting with her own money the three-story hospital that would serve her community for another forty years.

The first hospital in Chattanooga owned, operated and staffed by African Americans, the Walden Hospital was so successful that Dr. Emma Wheeler was able to pay off the construction debt in less than three years. Emma Wheeler practiced medicine, was a member of the Mountain City Medical Society, trained nurses, founded the Nurses Services Club and raised a family.

Dr. Emma Wheeler died in 1957, but her legacy as a pioneer for women, African Americans and equality in medical services is as strong in Chattanooga as the building that remains. Now apartments that serve the bustling and ever-growing University of Tennessee at Chattanooga community, the building and its heritage serve as a reminder of the change that powerful hope and commitment can bring.

THE UNIVERSITY OF TENNESSEE AT CHATTANOOGA

Established in 1886 as Grant College or Grant University, the community bordering McCallie Avenue has grown as its name has changed. Dedicated to education and supported by the community, the University of Chattanooga merged into the University of Tennessee system, its students learning in buildings that were once the mansions of the city's elite. The nearby Fortwood community was Chattanooga's first historic district, the site of a large Civil War fort with a moat; it is now home to families and college fraternities.

SWAIM'S JAIL

Chattanooga was the gem that each general wanted in his crown, and the leaders of both the Union and the Confederacy vied to control this city. The Tennessee River and the railroad lines made the city a strategic goal for soldiers and spies on each side, and as the stakes grew higher, soldiers formulated plans to infiltrate the Scenic City and capture its strongholds.

James Andrews and his raiders toured the city while staying at the Crutchfield House, and when their raid failed, their last days were spent in a hole at Swaim's Jail. In a building seemingly perched on a steep hill, dreams vanished, replaced by the squeaks of rodents and the stench of men with lost hope. A Provident insurance parking lot now rests over Swaim's Jail, the notorious trapdoor to the "hole" never to open again.

The jail on Lookout Street was a small brick building with a high, wooden fence. The steep slope of the hill accommodated a basement dungeon accessed only by a trapdoor with a street-level entrance and living quarters for the jailer's family on the top floor. When the captured raiders were brought to the jail, they were sent to the dark confines of the recesses that lay under the trapdoor. Battling rats, rancid food and wretches, the raiders plotted, awaiting the opportunity to escape.

When enemy troops closed in on the city, the prisoners were moved, only to be returned days later, their desire for escape heightened by the news that their leader was to be put to death, scheduled to be hanged for his treasonous raid. Befriended by the blacksmith William "Uncle Bill" Lewis, Andrews spent his last days writing farewell letters and his will as scaffolding was being erected outside Swaim's Jail. As the Union army advanced dangerously close to Chattanooga, James Andrews was sent to Atlanta, and his hanging was carried out on Peachtree Street on the same day that Federal troops commanded by Colonel James Negley began the first artillery onslaught on the strategic city.

SOLDIERS MEMORIAL AUDITORIUM

The Soldiers and Sailors Memorial Auditorium was built in 1924 to serve as the primary municipal auditorium and exhibition hall for Chattanooga and Hamilton County, paying special homage to the veterans of the community.

Designed by the iconic architect R.H. Hunt, the Memorial Auditorium's mission changed as the community grew. The flat floor and flexible seating gave the venue the range to accommodate events as diverse as boxing matches, roller derby games, ice shows, religious revivals, banquets and dances. The annual Cotton Ball event was held in the auditorium, and more recently, a hydraulic orchestra lift and lighting and sound system improvements have made it a desirable venue for performances, hosting events like *Grease*, *Riverdance* and notable musicians.

TIVOLI THEATER

The "Jewel of the South" sits grandly on Broad Street in Chattanooga. The ninety-year-old historic showplace opened in 1921, and the Tivoli's high domed ceiling, grand lobby and elegant foyer accentuated its place as a state-of-the-art facility, unique for its ability to host both silent movies and live performances.

A 1963 Benwood grant saved the Tivoli as television thinned its crowds, and placement on the National Register of Historic Places saved it from demolition. The City of Chattanooga preserved it during a 1989 restoration, and today its ornate chandelier sparkles with the sounds of the Chattanooga Symphony and Opera Association. Chattanooga children thrill at the Beaux-Arts style of décor, the Wurlitzer Piano and the history that graces the walls as they attend live performances in a building that has hosted generations of their ancestors.

The Tivoli Theater is a beautiful example of Chattanooga's historic celebration of the arts and has been home to performances for over eighty years.

The Union Depot was built in 1882, its proximity to the car sheds making the Ninth Street location a bustling hub for travelers.

UNION STATION AND KRYSTAL BUILDING

By agreement with Thomas Crutchfield, the Union Depot was built across from the Crutchfield House. Seemingly distant from the bustling riverfront, this depot became the center of a town that continued to grow. Prior to its twentieth-century demolition, the depot was the center of commerce, with the trains filling the warehouses, car barns and storefronts. Until it was relocated to Kennesaw, Georgia (formerly Big Shanty), the General was a popular tourist attraction, drawing visitors who had fallen in love with the adventure of the Great Locomotive Chase (see full story on page 124). The station has been replaced on today's skyline by the Krystal Building and Tallan Building, skyscrapers that look out over the city the General's Raiders sought to destroy.

PATTEN PARKWAY

The site of the first Coca-Cola bottling plant, the Patten Parkway was anchored by the Delmonico Hotel, or Hotel Ross, built in 1888. Known as Yesterday's to modern generations of music-loving Chattanoogans, the building that reverberated with music was once a hotel where the attorney William Jennings Bryan spent his last night. During the Scopes Monkey Trial, Bryan traveled to the famous Rhea County Courthouse from the Chattanooga hotel on the last day of his life.

The Rhea County Courthouse in Dayton, Tennessee, was the site of the trial of John Thomas Scopes, a County High School teacher tried for teaching the evolutionary principle that man descended from a lower order of animals. William Jennings Bryan gave his last efforts supporting the prosecution while Clarence Darrow and Arthur Garfield Hays unsuccessfully defended the teacher and the principles of evolution.

The area surrounding Patten Parkway still echoes with music as Chattanoogans of all ages enjoy music, food and entertainment in a Friday night tradition called Nightfall, celebrated at the nearby Market Street Pavilion and Miller Park Plaza. This area was once swampy ponds where women braved rattlesnakes as they washed their clothes. The Volunteer Building, Miller Park and Miller Plaza are now at the center of town, no longer on its dangerous outskirts.

The Hotel Patten, built at the intersection of Eleventh and Market Streets, was designed to rival the Read House as a first-class hotel. The Dixie Highway Association would find its roots in meetings held at this hotel, with a southern route from Detroit to Miami coming to fruition in 1927. Bustling with activity, the hotel also served to host the first radio program in the city as the WDOD (Dynamo of Dixie) program broadcast from the site until 1978, when the building began its transition to serve as residential retirement and subsidized housing.

CITY HALL

Renovating can be a challenge for anyone, whether a business, government or family, but Chattanooga's leadership got a remarkable surprise as the renovation of the city hall uncovered a time capsule. Buried one hundred years earlier by the 1907 Chattanooga General Council, the time capsule's discovery was an invigorating event for an administration celebrating the

This time capsule was found almost one hundred years after it was placed. After having been forgotten for generations, it was found during a two-year renovation.

successes of a revitalized city and looking forward to a new era with bright promise. The relics from the time capsule are on display in a city hall that celebrates its staff and citizens. With walls decorated with mementos of the city's rich history and the art of its present people, this building reflects the administration's commitment to a powerful past and strong future.

At the turn of the century, Chattanooga was the "Dynamo of Dixie," its mammoth manufacturing concerns supplying a nation while darkening the skies and city around them. The items in the time capsule reflect that commitment to industry, including a directory roster of Chattanooga Chamber of Commerce officers and board of directors, a roster of the Chattanooga Manufacturers Association, a directory of the chamber of commerce, pamphlets celebrating the industry of the city and a yearbook from the Chattanooga Manufacturers Association.

The air was clear and the mood was celebratory when members of the Littlefield administration opened the 1907 time capsule. The city celebrating the twenty-first century embraces its history while moving forward to create a community that is a haven for families, outdoor enthusiasts, adventurers and people who believe in making change.

The Customs House, built of Tennessee marble, was built to serve as the federal building, originally housing the post office and other federal services.

Guests to Chattanooga can visit city hall and see the relics from the 1907 time capsule while enjoying art created by city employees and displays reflective of Chattanooga's new era.

CUSTOMS HOUSE

The U.S. Bankruptcy Court is housed in a historic building that was once the federal post office, also home to other United States government offices. Built in the Richardsonian Romanesque style, the combinations of rough and smooth stone appear to be delicate despite the strength of the stone walls and the reserve of the government it serves.

BESSIE SMITH MUSEUM

"The Empress of Blues" was an orphan before she was nine, dancing to her brother Andrew's guitar playing at the White Elephant Saloon in Chattanooga, Tennessee. Elizabeth Smith barely knew her father, an Alabama preacher, and when her mother died it was Bessie Smith, young entertainer, who joined her brother earning a living "busking" as a singer and dancer on the streets of her African American community in Chattanooga, Tennessee.

She was only ten years old when her brother Clarence ran away from home to join the musical troupe led by Moss Stokes, and when he returned a few years later she was ready to audition, earning a spot in the troupe and a mentor in the popular blues vocalist Ma Rainey. Performing with celebrities like Louis Armstrong, Benny Goodman and other jazz and blues greats prepared Bessie for a 1923 opportunity to record with Columbia Records, and she was a success.

"Down Hearted Blues" was named one of the songs of the century and is listed as one of the five hundred songs that shaped the rock and roll genre. Her career soared when she began recording, but as it waxed and waned, Bessie Smith continued live performances until her untimely 1937 death. The power of the blues in her music may have been reflective of the pain and anguish of her life experiences, family losses compounded by the tragedy of a young widow and a stormy marriage with an abusive Jack Gee.

Bessie Smith was on the road to a comeback, sitting comfortably with her common-law husband Richard Morgan, when their Packard hit another car. The spirit of the blues was crushed by the weight and force of a tragic automobile accident. The power of her story may have contributed to an unfounded urban legend, holding that she died because she was turned away from a white Mississippi hospital. The truth is that after the amputation of her arm, the queen of crooning tunes didn't regain consciousness and slipped away, her death more peaceful than much of her life.

Bessie Smith's estranged husband, Jack Gee, bore such ill will that he prevented her from having custody of their adopted son and prevented there being a tombstone erected at her grave site. It was not until August 1970 that singer Janis Joplin and former housekeeper Juanita Green were able to erect a tombstone in the great musician's honor—decades after more than seven thousand mourners celebrated her life at a Philadelphia funeral.

The museum in the heart of the Ninth Street/Martin Luther King Jr. district that was Bessie's home is a place for teaching, cultural expression and the celebration of the African American community that was so integral to the growth and success of the vibrant city. The museum partners with schools to teach future generations lessons learned from the patchwork that is the history of Chattanooga, its African American community and its impact on the growth of the nation and the music that energized it.

WAREHOUSE ROW

Once housing up to eight warehouses straining with the merchandise fueling the industrial and business growth of the city, the Market Street site now is a destination point for visitors and residents seeking high-end retail outlets and restaurants. Featuring a food court that complements the retail offerings and supports the needs of downtown employees and traveling visitors alike, Warehouse Row is easily accessible to the CARTA Electric Shuttle routes and the Tennessee Valley Authority complex.

TERMINAL STATION AND "CHATTANOOGA CHOO-CHOO"

Conceived of by Donn Barber in 1900, the vision of the Terminal Station won acclaim in the Beaux-Arts Institute in Paris, France, when students were asked to create plans for a railroad station in an American city. Modified to include the dramatic effect of the dome, work on Chattanooga's Terminal Station began on the site of the former Stanton House on South Market Street.

Travelers moved through the Terminal Station to the catchy tune of Glenn Miller's famous song, "Chattanooga Choo-Choo." The once grand building was saved from the wrecking ball and transformed by local businessmen into a family complex combining hotel space, entertaining restaurants, sleeping train cars, an indoor ice-skating rink and a combination of history and marketable nostalgia that continue to entertain America's tourists and Chattanooga's families.

TERMINAL BREWHOUSE

Now a popular restaurant and home to locally brewed beer, this building next door to the passenger terminal near the intersection of Market and Main Streets was once owned by an African American porter. Porter Davis owned the building next door, a hotel in the flat iron style that catered to the working class traveling and working by rail.

Until his death, Porter Davis's extensive family did not know of his charitable efforts and the unrelenting, anonymous efforts that guided former prisoners to a new chance at a life. Whether they worked for a meal or a bed, the many men and women who found new, hopeful lives from his generosity didn't forget Porter Davis, and after his funeral, many of them were said to have shared those stories as the historic building became part of new histories for the men and women guided by Porter Davis.

MAIN STREET

The buffalo worked out the line; the Indian followed it; the white man followed the Indian; the wagon road and railroad take the same route: the mountains shut in here; the valleys stop here; Tennessee River must pass through here; fact is, don't you see, this is the funnel of the world.
—nineteenth-century Chattanooga attorney Benjamin "Rush" Montgomery, quoted in Chattanooga's Story *by John Wilson*

Originally known as Montgomery Avenue in deference to its stalwart supporter, Benjamin Rush Montgomery, Main Street bisected the downtown area just south of the Union Station and became a thriving, bustling area as commerce surrounding the railroads increased with the construction boom of the post–Civil War years.

Today, this same area is celebrating an artistic revitalization as philanthropic grants from familiar families subsidize the growth of a community that celebrates the arts, allowing regional artists to uplift their city through their vision and the dream of sharing their work with the public.

FERGER PLACE

Following the Civil War, the South was a place of renewal, reconstruction and, in some places, resentment. Sherman's trail of destruction left Atlanta with smoking cinders and singed spirits; it was not a city that welcomed northern industrialists, investors or developers.

Chattanooga was a city that had already struggled with its divided loyalties. The last state to secede, Tennessee's Scenic City was home to families who had already battled with conflicting loyalties, families who were able to put those differences aside to protect the integrity of the city that they held dear.

The sheer beauty surrounding Chattanooga drew sightseeing soldiers, generals and privates alike trekking up the mountain for pictures and daguerreotypes perched atop Sunset Rock and amid the geologic formations that seemed to defy gravity, representing the eons of natural elements and their work on the boulders whose solid lessons would continue to thrill and educate for years to come.

The rosters of Chattanooga's business and civic leadership during the generations after the war tell two tales that converge. The story of the men who fell in love with the city that they guarded, served in, fought for and wrote home about is a powerful one. Many of these men returned to their families in the North and brought both their loved ones and their businesses back to the city and the vistas that had captured their hopes.

In 1887, Edward Young Chapin and Fred Ferger followed the boom to Chattanooga, leading friends from their law school days and Indiana childhoods toward fortunes in the Scenic City. The Ferger brothers would join Chapin in fueling the construction boom, while their law school friend, Benjamin Franklin Thomas, would become one of the first bottlers of that unusually refreshing new beverage, Coca-Cola. Harry Scott Probasco, another Indiana friend, would also fall under the spell of the Chattanooga fervor, building a banking industry that would propel the city's fortunes for generations.

Fred and his brother Herman conceived of and built the first planned subdivision in the South, a graceful horseshoe of houses that would occupy 240 acres of land along Main Street on the outskirts of a new and bustling city. The Ferger Place Historic District lies on the eastern rim of downtown Chattanooga at the foot of Missionary Ridge. The collage of post-Victorian architectural styles stretches from Morningside Drive to Eveningside Drive in a cul-de-sac that personified the changing building styles of the new century and reflected the personal tastes and growing wealth of the business and civic leaders who called it home.

Chapter 2

THE NORTH SHORE OF THE TENNESSEE RIVER

MOCCASIN BEND

Chattanooga has been called the funnel of the South, as people trace the trails of the buffalo, the imprints of the Native American tribes and the trade of the rivers. Moccasin Bend is acclaimed as one of the best-preserved samples of archaeological remains in the Tennessee River Valley. Its archaeological sites show how pivotal the area was in the development of trade, communication, economics and political importance in the region during twelve thousand years of prehistory and history.

The Bend is where the Tennessee River meets the hard geology of the Cumberland Plateau. Seen from the peaks of Lookout Mountain, the imprint of an Indian shoe has been the strategic crossroads of the region during more than ten thousand years of recorded history. The rich bottomland made it a desirable home to ever-evolving tribes of man in the Paleo-Indian, Archaic, Woodland and Mississippian Periods before the land came alive with the sounds of Chief Dragging Canoe's warriors.

The home to the largest contiguous evidence of prehistoric and historic sites, the Bend represents the greatest achievements in human evolution. Those are reflected in the changes in weaponry, community living, trading, hunting, gathering, gardening and, finally, the innovation of a stratified sociopolitical structure based on kinship.

Following the 1540 contact with Spanish explorer Hernando de Soto, the Bend was known as the Dark and Bloody Ground and was used by Cherokee and Creek tribes for hunting and gathering but left for inhabitation by the

Moccasin Bend, named for its unusual shape reminiscent of the earliest inhabitants, is the site of archaeological remains dating back to fourteen thousand years ago and the Paleo-Indian Period.

ancient spirits. In 1775, the Chickamauga Cherokee tribes of the Appalachian Mountain areas sought refuge from the white colonial aggression and encroachment. The last battle of the American Revolution was fought above the Bend at the Cravens House on September 20, 1782. During that final skirmish, the Cherokee, who had aligned themselves with the British after their homes were destroyed by frontiersmen, avenged themselves against their aggressors and settled into the valley they had revered before as dark and bloody ground.

Chief Dragging Canoe and the Chickamauga Cherokee he led moved here to flee white colonial aggression. They shifted to farmsteading, embracing individual ownership of one square mile per head of household. This move to a more agrarian lifestyle was a calculated effort to appease the increasing numbers of white settlers, and Chief Dragging Canoe's community grew to include seven villages along the river.

As the numbers of flatboats migrating through the Tennessee River increased, Chief Dragging Canoe's warriors took up their bows against pioneers stuck in the raging waters of the Suck, the Boiling Pot and the Frying Pan, lying under their mountain vantage points to dissuade the migrating pioneers from taking root in their land.

Tomorrow's children will enjoy the 780-acre Moccasin Bend National Archaeological District, as the plans of the Friends of Moccasin Bend National Park and the support of the United States Congress turn the hope for a valley's past into an area that the future can enjoy. Supporting the highest level of preservation, protection, management and interpretation, the cultural, historic and natural resources of the national park will entertain and educate future generations of Americans.

Brown's Ferry and Brown's Tavern

The Great Warpath and the Great Trading Path come into the Chattanooga Valley as a single path, diverging at the area we know as Reflection Riding. The Warpath went toward Ooltewah, and the Trading Path went across the river at Brown's Ferry and Williams Island, north along Walden's Ridge.

In 1803, John Brown, the mixed-blood son of Richard Brown, built Brown's Ferry Tavern to serve as a resting stop for travelers crossing the Cherokee nation. His tavern linked the Brown's Ferry at Moccasin Bend with the Brown's Ferry at Williams Island that he operated with his father, Richard Brown. The tavern was a popular resting place for travelers from Nashville, and rumor had it that many met an untimely end at the hands of the innkeeper.

Chief John Ross and his wife, Quatie, a relative of John Brown, are said to have spent their honeymoon at the tavern, now the oldest house in Hamilton County, two hundred years after its foundation was laid.

His tavern was used as a warehouse for federal troops during the war, and while he left with his family in the Cherokee removal, John Brown returned to his land in the 1840s and, according to legend, is buried somewhere on the 347 acres of farmland around his tavern.

The archaeological sites at Williams Island and Moccasin Bend show contiguous occupation and reflect the changes in the evolution of man's abilities as he moved from primitive weapons toward a nation that embraced agriculture, sociopolitical advances and all of the stages of evolution marking the path from the Paleo-Indian, Archaic, Woodland and Mississippian Periods.

Today, the same land at Williams Island is home to an organic farm, sustaining a community effort and providing a unique opportunity for education.

WILLIAMS ISLAND

An ancient guardian of the entrance to the Tennessee River Gorge, Williams Island sits in the middle of the Tennessee River, a 450-acre island formed by silt built up in the middle of the channel. Farmed continuously for more than one thousand years, the island is two miles long and shows evidence of sixteenth-century Spanish trade artifacts, AD 1000 Mississippian-era villages and earlier sites dating back to 12,000 BC.

Williams Island was the site of the Tuskegee Town, headquarters to its chief, Bloody Fellow, during 1776. Half-blood John Brown operated a ferry to the island during the early 1800s. Bloody Fellow was convinced by the Scottish trader, John McDonald, not to kill a young trader new to the territory. Daniel Ross, the young trader accompanying the Chickasaw chief Piomingo's goods, would be convinced by McDonald to join him and became father to the great Cherokee chief John Ross.

Following the Indian removal and the Trail of Tears, Samuel Williams acquired the island, but the wealthy plantation owner lived in hiding during much of the Civil War after his discovery of the leader of the Andrews's Raiders clinging naked to the shore. Hunted by Union soldiers and derided by Confederate stalwarts, Sam Williams had been called the "father of Chattanooga" for his enthusiastic support of Chattanooga's growth. A merchant, land speculator and city booster, Williams struggled when he found James Andrews on his island, his sympathy further bolstered by the story that the hijacking wasn't driven by patriotism but by the reward money that would ensure Andrews a safe return to his sweetheart.

The advance of Federal troops required the removal of Andrews and the other captured and recaptured raiders to Atlanta, where Conductor Fuller reported that Andrews "died bravely." As Chattanooga changed hands and the Federal soldiers billeted in his home, a brave Samuel Williams took refuge under a rock on his island, hiding there for brief visits with his wife, their conversation muffled from the Union soldiers by his daughters playing the piano.

The brave Williams further enraged the Union generals by serving the Confederate army as a guide, but he was granted immunity by the Reconstruction president, Andrew Johnson, after his wife was given an audience to the man they had known previously as their tailor in Greeneville, Tennessee.

THE BAYLOR SCHOOL

Professor John Roy Baylor brought his enthusiasm for education to Chattanooga from Virginia and started the Baylor School for Boys at the McCallie family homestead in 1893. He was brought here by prominent citizens eager to offer quality education to their children. The $100 yearly tuition for the school was the highest rate of any school in the state and replaced the University School, establishing itself at a new Palmetto street address.

Supported by the J.T. Lupton family and other prominent Chattanoogans, the Baylor School for Boys established itself on a campus across from Williams Island near the base of Signal Mountain. The tradition of excellence continues today, and now coeducational, the Baylor School consistently ranks among the top private schools in the country, offering boarding students from dozens of countries the opportunity to achieve an education in a setting with natural beauty as its backdrop.

OLGIATI BRIDGE

Named for the mayor who presided during its construction, the P.R. Olgiati Bridge is downstream from the Walnut Street and Market Street spans. Crossing the Tennessee River downstream from the downtown traffic, the Olgiati Bridge connects to the freeway north across Stringer's Ridge toward Signal Mountain, Red Bank and parts north.

HILL CITY

Its name reflects the topographical challenges of the North Chattanooga neighborhood known prior to annexation as "Hill City." Houses perched atop cliffs and driveways that seem to defy gravity compete for views that are so breathtaking as to be worth the effort.

Alleys bisect streets at improbable angles and narrow streets wind along crests, cliffs and ridges that seem better suited to the goats that eat the kudzu than to the cars that hug the edges. Named for General Nathan Bedford Forrest, a street winds through the neighborhood, losing an "R" around one curve and gaining it back in another as gentrification and development challenge history. Street signs over the years have taken away the letter that would identify the place with the man and made the suggestion that a general lauded for his military success and personal accomplishments should lose his place in history for the actions and shame brought to his name by followers.

FRAZIER AVENUE

Captain S.J.A. Frazier was a Confederate soldier who was wounded during the Chickamauga campaign and found solace in the area north of the Tennessee River. Following his recuperation, Frazier purchased seventy acres along the shore. His name continues to adorn a street that is alive with families and energy and is home to restaurants, shops, public art and entertainment in an eclectic neighborhood combining history with future. It is marked by brass dance steps that encourage visitors to connect with one another while embracing the neighborhood's experience.

STRINGER'S RIDGE

Three hills, known to the Hill City locals below as "Old Baldy," make up Stringer's Ridge, a view so strategic that it was the site of the first Union invasion of Chattanooga. Brigadier General James S. Negley's forces bombarded Chattanooga from this ridge on June 7, 1862, as faithful congregants worshipped below. The following year, Stringer's Ridge was again the base of Union mortars assaulting the city below as the Indiana Battery of General Wilder's Brigade opened the Chickamauga Campaign with two weeks of relentless bombarding.

The Confederate forces controlled the city until Wilder's Brigade took the ridge named for Captain William Stringer, a veteran of the Seminole and Mexican Wars. The highest points of the ridge still contain Civil War earthworks, and Chattanoogans who explore the hiking trails and winding paths owe thanks to the dedication of the Tennessee River Gorge Trust and the generosity of Chattanooga developers.

The Stringer family operated the Beason Ferry at what is now called Renaissance Park, a unique wetland park that heralds a new era of land conservation and responsible management of public resources. In 1908, Stringer's Ridge again resonated with the booming sounds of war when construction began on a three-hundred-foot-long tunnel. Excavated with mostly convict labor, the tunnel's crew battled cave-ins on the south side as they proceeded, without a tunnel expert, until it was completed in March 1911.

DELTA QUEEN

Launched from a California port in 1925 the steamboat *Delta Queen* had a proud past before its 2009 relocation to Chattanooga's Coolidge Park. The home to a celebrated ghost, a captain still watching over its charge, the *Delta Queen* was designated a National Historic Landmark in 1989 and was inducted into the National Maritime Hall of Fame in 2004. Following service as a barracks for the United States Navy, the California vessel traversed American waterways, adding a calliope (or steam) organ, and battled legislative changes to keep serving as a floating hotel.

The *Delta Queen*, one of the last paddleboats on the Tennessee River, now finds its home at Coolidge Park. Known for its captain, a woman of such strength that her ghostly spirit continues to watch over it, the *Delta Queen* hosts hotel rooms, dining areas and live music. *Courtesy of Joseph Hookey.*

CHATTANOOGA THEATRE CENTRE

Founded in 1923, the Chattanooga Theatre Centre is one of the oldest, largest and busiest community theatre programs in the country. For almost one hundred years, the theatre has been the center of a lively, creative performing arts community boasting as many as fifteen productions each year.

The forty-thousand-square-foot facility on the Tennessee River both teaches and entertains, its education outreach programs supporting learning through partnerships with local schools, the University of Tennessee at Chattanooga and Chattanooga State Technical Community College. The 380-seat main stage hosts grand productions supported by state-of-the-art dressing areas, rehearsal halls and workrooms. The enthusiasm of the patrons keeps a lively schedule of smaller performances in the 200-seat Circle stage.

COOLIDGE PARK

Lush grass, trees celebrating Chattanooga's international sister cities and a fountain with water features adorn a riverfront that, until 1999, was littered with scrap metal and the detritus of an abandoned shipping yard. As the spirit of revitalization swept through the North Shore, it created a path toward a brighter future for a city that had been dimmed by pollution and ravaged by unfettered manufacturing.

An 1894 Dentzel carousel became the central feature of the revitalization of the shipping yard as the public and private partnerships that had come to characterize change in Chattanooga turned the riverfront eyesore into a mecca for families and the heart of a new North Shore community alive with festivals, events and celebrations. Named for Technical Sergeant Charles H. Coolidge, a Signal Mountain resident, the twenty-two-acre park celebrates Coolidge's extraordinary heroism during World War II that earned him the Congressional Medal of Honor.

The antique carousel featuring fifty-two hand-carved animals, a calliope band organ and ornate gold leaf benches brings Chattanooga children a glimpse of the past alongside the historic lines and sounds of the *Delta Queen* and the *Southern Belle*. Chattanooga families thrill to the sounds of festivals, parties and picnics along the riverfront under the panorama of the historic bridges, magnificent bluffs and lush, wooded island.

RENAISSANCE PARK

The Civil War brought great change to the area along the Tennessee River. The Confederate troops built forts near the river in 1862, and Union forces began building sawmills and ship repair facilities on the river upon their 1863 arrival. Escaped slaves from all over the region lived at what we now call Renaissance Park, then called Camp Contraband. These former slaves provided labor on Union construction projects, and many in the camp enlisted in the United States Colored Troops. A November 1865 census calculated the camp's population at nearly 3,500; it was a community of its own growing on the river's edge.

A series of city Civil War interpretive signs is located in the park on the north bank across the Market Street Bridge.

Camp Contraband—This was the site of a large camp of ex-slaves liberated by Union occupation of the area.

1864 Military Bridge—The Union army constructed a wooden bridge here, the first to cross the river.

Union Blockhouse – The foundation remains of a Union-built blockhouse that protected the bridge here during the war.

United States Colored Troops—This area was also used as a campground for the USCT. By the end of the war, more than 24,000 black troops had served in Tennessee. They were first employed as laborers and guards but also saw combat, suffering nearly 4,500 casualties during the war.

THE GIRLS' PREPARATORY SCHOOL (GPS)

Three teachers from Chattanooga High School combined their efforts to form the Girls' Preparatory School in 1906. It opened in a frame building near the courthouse square at Oak and Lindsey Streets. Four teachers staffed the school during its opening year; one of the founders was the sister of the McCallie School family. Growing to a larger campus across the Tennessee River, the school would become an icon of education celebrated for its role in providing women in Chattanooga with an exemplary education.

THE BRIGHT SCHOOL

Mary Gardner Bright, ancestor of the Bright family still represented in Chattanooga today, began an elementary school in 1913 to support the families preparing their children to attend Baylor, McCallie or GPS. Outgrowing its original McCallie Avenue address, the Bright School also moved across the river. Its enrollment included the most historic and prominent Chattanooga families.

NORMAL PARK

Nestled in a quiet neighborhood is a building whose arrival was accompanied by a mighty procession. Proud Chattanoogans and Hill City residents marched triumphantly from Market Street across the Walnut Street Bridge to the nine acres of land holding the promise of hope for their city's future: a business, commercial and literary university.

The escort for the deputy grandmaster included over fifty Knights Templar, members of the Lookout commandery. The *Chattanooga Times* described the Masonic procession as carrying drawn swords, rods, squares,

The laying of the cornerstone for the Normal University, now home to Normal Park Museum Magnet School, was celebrated by a Masonic procession from Ninth Street to the Mississippi Avenue site.

levels and plumbs, the tools of their ancient trade, and silver and golden vessels bearing the oil, wine and corn used in the blessing of the cornerstone. The grandmaster of the oldest lodge represented carried the book of constitutions on September 15, 1896, as the procession marched toward the site of the Normal College.

The Chattanoogans who marched to celebrate the coming of the college spent their days with a different skyline than do we. Their eyes saw Lookout Mountain's smaller twin instead of the reflective lines of Cameron Hill's newest residents, BlueCross BlueShield. The Walnut Street Bridge was a new conveyance over the still-raging Tennessee River, and the only skyscraper on the horizon was the Dome Building, the golden-topped home of the *Chattanooga Times*. This was a town still struggling to overcome the wrath of the Civil War, and its people were passionate about industry and education.

During the industrial boon, Chattanooga was the "Dynamo of Dixie," its community also fostering the educational institutions that would teach its youth the business and leadership skills to keep their city's path clear. Chattanooga University and the Baylor School were both in their infancy, toddlers that would grow to become the landmark University of Tennessee at Chattanooga and a nationally recognized preparatory school when ground was broken for the Normal College in Chattanooga's neighboring Hill City.

A front yard that now boasts an imposing but whimsical metal dinosaur has sloped toward a quiet, tree-lined street while Chattanooga has chased its dream of success, annexing the community called Hill City, merging school systems and moving toward the future those early boosters dreamed of.

Founded in 1859, the Normal School in Valpariaso, Indiana, was the largest of its kind by 1891 and sought in Chattanooga a southern campus to expand its mission of normal education. Leaders heralded that the "foundation has been laid for making of Chattanooga the greatest education center as well as the most important industrial city in the South."

"Normal" indicated to educators a university system that taught a core of subjects, with emphasis on additional categories that inspired the student and provided a base upon which to found a career in business, science, teaching or music. "Man is greater than his surroundings if he develops himself. The greatest world is at the little end of the telescope."

Though the bricks would change names as the college was sold to the county and then transferred to the city, that name "Normal" has remained, attached so oddly to a building that has inspired an unrelenting enthusiasm for education that is extraordinary. In 1926, the parents of Normal Park School sponsored a program heralded as an important step in pioneering early childhood education, a program now called kindergarten.

Proponents of Normal Park called its revolutionary class "School Before Six" and, buoyed by the energies of a remarkable teacher and an organized group of parents, organized programs in local churches and took the message of their mission to the representatives, lobbying every legislator they could find. Their goal would not be met until 1971, but the enthusiasm and support of the parents didn't waver.

During World War II, Chattanoogans read with pride of the efforts of the small school and its PTA as they managed the dismantling of a 135-foot water tower that weighed 54,125 pounds for the city newspaper's scrap contest. "The total of 226,250 pounds of scrap we have accumulated is attributable to the teamwork of the children of Normal Park School, the teachers and the P.T.A." The newspaper's words of congratulations were printed alongside reports of American subs sinking enemy ships and missing local soldiers, the success of the children and families made more powerful by the war that they supported.

The halls in that unassuming building have echoed for generations with the sounds of children, their teachers and the parents who supported the mission, a magical mix that continues to prove that a community serves itself best by teaching its children. A yellowed newspaper article in the school's archives describes the community's response to a "Help Wanted" sign sent home with each student, a plea to members of the community to share their time tutoring children, a program that succeeded and laid the seed for a school that has consistently received national honors.

A 1940 alumnus remembers his aunt's description of the site as an old fort where families had picnics. Now that grassy lawn bustles with activity, a regular stop for educators and legislators, famous for the success of its model and legendary for the power of its people and its partnerships. Arts organizations, museums, businesses and foundations dedicated to education partner with the staff and parents of Normal Park to send their children into the world armed with the enthusiastic love of learning that makes a person a leader.

The name "Normal" may be a goal that has so powerfully moved the parents, neighbors, community members and leaders who have worked to make an extraordinary education normal for all of its students. The staff, teachers and parents reflect the cultural and economic diversity that characterize the neighborhood, but they share a passion for their children, community and city. Their work is reflected as powerfully in the glow of the smiles of the students and teachers as in the shining metal of the awards and recognitions.

Lyndhurst

The Riverview home of the bottling magnate J.T. Lupton, Lyndhurst was built on the north bank of the Tennessee River. Originally the site of the Beck family farm, the mansion anchored one side of the large property. Its opposite side was home to the Chattanooga Golf and Country Club. Union supporters whose father came to Chattanooga in 1822, Joshua and David Beck operated a quarry that supplied stone for many of the significant buildings in early Chattanooga.

Chapter 3

LOOKOUT MOUNTAIN

FOREST HILLS CEMETERY

Forest Hills Cemetery sits at the base of Lookout Mountain, the beginning of the fertile Chattanooga valley. Founded 130 years ago, this "homestead" of the dead has been the resting place of some of Chattanooga's most famous citizens, their shadows heavy over monuments that tell the story of the Scenic City.

Once each spring, the "dead" stroll Forest Hills' lush green lawns, and azaleas and dogwoods decorate a day that is alive with history. Today's Chattanoogans don the personas of the men and women who shaped much of the future of the city they all called home.

Hundred-Acre Homage

Southern cities and their families celebrate the resting place of their ancestors in a way that is a unique blend of many cultural traditions. In the South, cemeteries are places where families might have picnics, taking flowers to their deceased grandmother on her birthday or playing Frisbee to commemorate her neighboring husband on Grandparent's Day. For southern families, these settings aren't just places for mourning; often, they are sites for reflective celebrations and an excuse for elders to share teachings from the lives of those who came before.

At Forest Hills, familial love and community pride are an art form set in the stone, marble and statuary of a hundred-acre homage to the people who carved a thriving city out of a wilderness trading post.

Colonel Abraham Malone Johnson established this pastoral resting place as he was developing an area he called St. Elmo, named in homage to a novel that glorified Chattanooga's bravery during the Civil War. That place is now home to more than forty-seven thousand souls, and the massive oak trees that tower above the cemetery grounds have been protective sentries, growing taller and wider with the flock they've guarded since 1880.

During its early years, the city of Chattanooga fell victim to diseases like cholera and consumption, and their ravages are recorded on the tombstones and monuments of Forest Hills. There, the names of forgotten children from the Vine Street orphanage can be found alongside the names of famous Civil War officers, renowned entertainers and the business leaders and families who turned their sleepy town into a bustling, turn-of-the-century city.

Where the City's Past Sleeps

Colonel A.M. Johnson was married to the daughter of one of the first developers of Chattanooga, Colonel James Whiteside. Following in the entrepreneurial spirit of his father-in-law, Johnson built one of the early turnpikes up Lookout Mountain. Both men were eventually laid to rest in the shadow of the mountain.

Also buried in Forest Hills is Harriet Whiteside, James's wife, an iconic female figure in Chattanooga's history. After the Civil War, she paid the taxes on her home atop Lookout Mountain by charging a twenty-five-cent entry fee for that famous, scenic view—a toll enforced by shotgun-wielding men.

By Johnson's death in 1903, Chattanooga was a booming hub of the South, attracting many men who brought their families, businesses and entrepreneurial spirit to the Scenic City, and whose tombs can be found at Forest Hill.

The cemetery is home to Garnet Carter, Rock City's founder and the inventor of miniature golf; Joe Engel, "the Barnum of Baseball" and Engel Stadium namesake; actress and opera singer Grace Moore, the "Tennessee Nightingale"; baseball phenom Jackie Mitchell, the girl who struck out Babe Ruth; Joseph Cadek, founder of the Cadek Conservatory of Music; and four U.S. senators, six congressmen and other amazing Chattanoogans.

Visiting Forest Hills

One day a year, the serene beauty of the Forest Hills Cemetery is the backdrop of a montage of live performances as actors and descendants celebrate some of the personages buried there. In costume and character, these dedicated enthusiasts take guests back in time, drawing them into the lives of people who on other days are just names etched onto Gothic or Victorian monuments decorated with Biblical figures or ancient gods.

Pack a picnic—or just an appetite for history—and visit Forest Hills Cemetery with your family. If you can't make it in person to enjoy the breathing reincarnations of our city's lively spirits, download the cemetery's brochure at ForestHillsCemetery.net. (Click on News & Events, and then scroll to the bottom of the page and click on the scroll brochure.) Then take your own family on the tour, learning together as you enjoy a beautiful day with pretty flowers, interesting scenes and history that can come alive before your eyes.

INCLINE

The view from Lookout Point has drawn people for centuries, the majestic scene bringing seven states to the fore, a thin line in the distance separating land from sky. But once upon a time that view was blocked, guarded by armed sentries, as a battle waged over toll roads up the mountain—a battle led by the feisty widow of one of Chattanooga's founders, James A. Whiteside.

Colonel James A. Whiteside was one of the founding fathers of the Scenic City. His family is featured in the famous portrait of Moccasin Bend still hanging in the Hunter Museum.

Colonel Whiteside came to Chattanooga in 1838. The vibrant thirty-five-year-old attorney from Pikeville, Tennessee, had already served in the state legislature for over a decade. He purchased large tracts of land in Chattanooga, heralding growth and building in what had been a small trading post, and is credited with bringing the railroads to Chattanooga.

Whiteside's fine home on Cameron Hill was the first brick building in the city, built by fellow newcomer and leading citizen Thomas Crutchfield Sr. The colonel also owned extensive land on Lookout Mountain, developing a road up the mountain called Summertown and later obtaining a charter for a toll road, Whiteside Pike, to bring the wonders and beauty of the mountain within reach of the traveling public.

Whiteside became known as "Old Man Chattanooga" and "Old Man Lookout Mountain." His family portrait, now hanging in the Hunter Museum, is the first known depiction of the view from that majestic mountain, overlooking a valley that Whiteside himself helped build. Though he died in 1861 bringing his wounded son home from the Civil War, his legacy continues to live on in others' appreciation of the wonders of Lookout Mountain.

Widow's Peak?

In a town known for its Choo Choo, perhaps it was inevitable that tourists' appreciation of Lookout Mountain resulted in the world's most famous incline railway. But the Incline we know today is not the original. "America's Most Amazing Mile" had three incarnations—some hindered and some helped by Colonel Whiteside's widow.

Harriet Whiteside and her gun-wielding guards went all the way to the Supreme Court to defend their right to charge for a view from the point. Her win, adjudicated by Judge David M. Key, prompted her competitors to build the first incline to their mountaintop hotel from St. Elmo, avoiding the Whitesides' property and toll road.

Lookout Incline Railway Company took its first passengers up its narrow-gauge line on what would later be called Incline No. 1 on March 10, 1887. A broad-gauge railway began operation on May 29, 1888, carrying passengers from downtown Chattanooga to the top of Lookout Mountain and back for the princely sum of twenty-five cents. Passengers must have had white knuckles as their car was locked, hanging to the tracks on top of the mountain, waiting for the engine to perform its switchback action and take them on the next leg of their journey. At the time, it was the only known switchback in the South.

Lookout Mountain

Battlefield Ends War

Not to be outdone, Harriet Whiteside financed another incline to carry passengers 4,750 feet with giant cables and steam power. Imagine sitting in a small, windowed car and climbing nine-tenths of a mile straight up a mountain. As Chattanoogans, we are sometimes immune to the novelty and excitement that is the breathless trip up our beloved mountain; close your eyes and consider making that same, improbable trip over a century ago.

Incline No. 2 broke ground in August 1895 and made its first trip up the mountain in November of the same year. Conceived of by J.T. Crass, the contractor who came to Chattanooga to build the roads of the Chickamauga Battlefield Park, this incline became a vital transportation link for the residents of Lookout Mountain, hauling building supplies, coal, groceries and people up the 72.7 percent grade.

With cars that still climb to an altitude of 2,100 feet above sea level, the second incline's completion was timed to coincide with the dedication of the Chickamauga-Chattanooga National Military Park. The controversy over the rights to the point view was resolved when Chattanooga icons Adolph Ochs and Alexander W. Chambliss worked to incorporate that land into the newly created military park system.

Meanwhile, yet another incline served Cameron Hill, which at that time was the more diminutive image of its neighbor, Lookout Mountain. Operated by the Chattanooga Water Power Company, the Cameron Hill Incline Company took passengers up the hill along Fourth Street, traversing that five-block stretch between 1889 and 1896.

Marvel of Engineering

Chattanooga is home to the steepest passenger incline railway in the world, and presidents, princes, publishers, generals and Americans of all kinds have thrilled at climbing those heights.

Chief Dragging Canoe's lookouts may have taken days to climb to the point, searching for pioneers—potential victims of the Tennessee River Gorge's powerful "Suck" or their warriors' spears. But the Incline, a marvel of engineering using cables five thousand feet long and, since 1912, two one-hundred-horsepower motors, carries passengers up Lookout Mountain, without incident, in less than fifteen minutes. Our own Incline Railway is still hailed internationally as the steepest and safest of its kind.

CRAVENS HOUSE

Halfway up Lookout Mountain on the Georgia side, the Cravens House is tucked away, a right turn that can take you back in history to remnants from the prehistoric Woodland Period and past massive trees whose leaves may have rustled as the Cherokee and frontiersmen fought what is known as the last battle of the Revolutionary War on September 20, 1782. The Chickamauga warriors fought with the British and after the 1779 destruction of their villages. The last battle was waged when Chief Wyuka and his Chickamauga Indians met John Sevier and his militia guns flared.

This same land became home to the Robert Cravens family when he built a house known as the "White House" in 1857. A pioneer iron manufacturer, Robert Cravens was a leader in Chattanooga industry, and his house was rebuilt in 1867 after the ravages of the Civil War.

Before it became popular for industrialists to build summer homes for their families atop the cooler mountain, Robert Cravens built a home that he called Alta Vista, ensconcing his family in a home that was "high and beautiful," one of the first homes on the mountain to be occupied year-round.

The Confederates used the circles and wall for protection during the early hours of the Battle of Lookout, but archaeological evidence suggests that the history of the stone structures dates back to the prehistoric Woodland Period over ten thousand years ago. The property was commandeered as an observation point by the Confederate army during the early part of the war, and after sharing quarters with the regiment commanded by General Walthall, the family moved to their farm near Ringgold. When they returned after the war, the Union soldiers who had gained control of the strategic observation station had gutted the house, leaving the family only a skeleton with stone chimneys.

BATTLE ABOVE THE CLOUDS

The highlight of the three-thousand-acre Lookout Mountain Battlefield is Point Park, which overlooks Chattanooga and the bending Tennessee River.

Confederates defended this seemingly impregnable position following the Battle of Chickamauga in September 1863. With Confederates on these and other heights and blocking roads and railroads entering the city, the Union army was in trouble, hunkering down in the city. But Federal reinforcements arrived, and a slender supply line opened in late October. General U.S.

Battle of Lookout Mountain depicts the bloody battle over the foggy crest of the mountain, a strategic point that generals from both sides wanted to control.

Grant, placed in overall command in Chattanooga, ordered assaults on the Confederate positions in late November. Aided by a heavy fog on the mountain, Union attacks on November 24 against Confederate positions on Lookout Mountain were successful.

The next day, similar attacks on Missionary Ridge also won success. The Confederate stranglehold on Chattanooga had ended. General Braxton Bragg, who commanded the Confederate army at Chickamauga and Chattanooga, resigned after the defeats. He was replaced by General Joseph Johnston, who consolidated his defeated army in north Georgia to await developments. The Union army turned Chattanooga into a vast supply depot and used the city as a base for future operations in Georgia.

The Lookout Mountain Visitor Center is located across the street from Point Park. James Walker's thirteen- by thirty-three-foot painting *Battle of*

Lookout Mountain is displayed there with a short narrative of the fighting. It is open daily from 8:30 a.m. to 5:00 p.m.

The Cravens House, home to early Chattanooga industrialist Robert Cravens, was the site of some of the heaviest fighting during the Lookout Mountain battle. The house and grounds are located below the point. The grounds are open year-round (free admission). The house is open for tours during the summer. Call for hours.

See the Lookout Mountain Unit map on the park's website (www.nps. gov/chch) for more features of the site.

FAIRYLAND CLUB AND ROCK CITY

Mist, marvels, magic and mystery—all have lived on a mountaintop above our valley. Even now, spirits may waft in ghostly shapes on nights lit by a bright moon, floating over boulders whose very shapes and precarious placements defy our understanding and expand our idea of the nature of time.

The most famous ghost stories of the mountain come from its earliest inhabitants. Some say the haunting souls of a young couple hover above the waterfall at Rock City's Lover's Leap, or "High Falls." According to legend, a Native American man loved a woman from another tribe. Her people, blinded by the rage of their intolerance, threw him from that ledge—and then watched in horror as their own daughter jumped to her death, honoring her vow of love. Families driving up the Ochs Highway extension may still hear the screams of that lost couple, whistling through the crevices between the rocks on Lookout Mountain.

"Dark and Bloody" History

The birth of the mountain was itself violent. Imagine, though, the terrible roar as tectonic plates crashed over two hundred million years ago, earthquakes sending the bed of an ancient sea rising to the sky, forming that mountain with crevices and fissures that would erode to become the waterfalls, caves and marvels that have enthralled and educated generations of people.

Native Americans called the valley below Lookout Mountain the "Dark and Bloody Ground"—and that was long before the Civil War soaked the soil with the blood of hundreds of thousands of Americans. Native people considered the valley a land offered by their gods as fertile hunting ground, not a place to dwell; it was, they thought, inhabited by the spirits of their

Lookout Mountain

Umbrella Rock is just one of the amazing natural works of art that can be seen atop Lookout Mountain. Rock City Gardens celebrates those natural formations and the flora indigenous to the Tennessee Valley.

ancestors, who would guide hunters to feed ongoing generations. The people respected and feared the spirits of their Dark and Bloody Ground.

Looming above the valley, Lookout Mountain and its famous profile were a destination point for travelers through many ages. They followed paths worn deep by buffalo, hunters, warriors, families and, later, trains, cars and more families. The panoramic view lured men in moccasins, pioneers and soldiers. Were they drawn by the strategic advantage of the view of seven states or enraptured by the breathtaking vista?

Caves Link Past, Present

The area's haunted past extends from Lookout Valley to the mountain's peak—and even to within Lookout Mountain itself. In the miles of caves that honeycomb the mountain, native shamans and chiefs held tribal conferences, and warriors hid caches of weapons and loot from their bloodthirsty raids.

Some of those caves, now part of Rock City, are stages to gnomes and figures depicting European folk tales. These scenes, whose appeal has

While waiting for the golf course atop Lookout Mountain to be completed, Rock City's developer casually picked up a stick and invented miniature golf to entertain his guests.

spanned generations of children, are set in caves that took millions of years to create. Those caves were preserved and, since 1932, made public by the caretakers of the land, Garnet and Frieda Carter.

Mrs. Carter relished the natural beauty of the mountain and was passionate about sharing it with others. Her imagination was inflamed by the almost fanciful way some boulders, heavy enough to crush a car, seemed to balance on their tips. The shapes she imagined in other boulders—monolithic examples of geological upheaval and eons of erosion—are a testament to the engaging spirit of a woman who preserved part of a geological heritage that few Americans are lucky enough to share.

Mr. Carter dreamed of developing a residential neighborhood on top of the mountain at a time when air quality was sending people to higher land. His indulgence of his wife's love of the flora and natural art of the mountaintop became more acute as word spread about the beauty of their property. A natural salesman, he saw entrance fees in the eyes of the people who asked to visit "Miss Frieda's garden."

Wonder and awe are around every corner, and as the vistas take a guest's breath away the enormity of the history of the caves, formations and fantasy inspire. Amid the boulders and the winding path Garnet Carter invented the game of miniature golf, hitting a ball with a shortened stick as a lark as he waited with friends for the golf course to be completed.

Haunted Fairyland

The community Garnet Carter developed is still called Fairyland, a neighborhood built around its natural wonder, not through it. Since 1924, the epicenter of the community has been the Fairyland Club, a building in the English Tudor Revival style that is now included in the National Register of Historic Places. Some may think ghosts and ghouls frolic on the mountaintop only in October, when Ruby Falls and Rock City celebrate Halloween, but rumor has it that the Fairyland Club has two year-round ghosts of its own.

Built from local stone, with stucco and steep timbering, the Fairyland Club is a fascinating building, riddled with nooks and crannies; its walls and grounds have been haven to generations of families whose fortunes guided the future of Chattanooga.

It's also been a haven to Bobby, a persnickety ghost who is said to lurk in one of the ladies' rooms. Reputedly the thwarted lover in a deadly romantic triangle, Bobby announces his presence to ladies by breathing down their necks; he smells of cigarette smoke. Some women have reported accounts of him slamming doors, flapping the restroom stalls and throwing tissue boxes. Another spirit said to inhabit the Fairyland Club is that of a young woman. Rumor has it she frequents the offices there, and prom groups who book the building have been known to leave her a seat at the table.

At the Fairyland Club, as on all of Lookout Mountain, there are plenty of ghosts to go around.

Natural Bridge

Extending sixty feet long and hovering fifteen feet above the ground, the Natural Bridge on Lookout Mountain might have seemed to early settlers and ancient Indian tribes like a toy left by a giant or god. It is a mystery of Mother Nature.

The bridge's geological neighbor, Telephone Rock, is also a marvel, a mammoth boulder with a hole that conveys sound from one side to another,

Set in a wooded ravine, the Natural Bridge is still the perfect place to celebrate nature's wonder with children, the grotto providing shade, fun and a fascinating example of geology.

like a telephone. Two other formations, known as the "Old Man of the Mountain" and the "Chinese Grin," sit atop Lookout Mountain, their comical countenances etched by millions of years of weather, wind and rain.

In a time when children have remarkable technology at their fingertips, the geological absurdity of these strangely shaped boulders offers a lesson in the effects of time and weather that pairs nicely with a family outing and a Frisbee.

The Natural Bridge area, especially, is both geographically fascinating and rich in history. The land around it, a plot now divided by Bragg Avenue at the corner of Scenic Highway, was the site of salubrious springs, state-of-the-art schools, spiritualist camps and even séances.

Healing Waters

In 1878, the rusty chalybeate springs that ran under the Natural Bridge brought desperate Chattanoogans up the mountain, racing to escape a yellow fever epidemic that was consuming downtown. The people climbed toward the healing mineral waters to camp among the boulders at what is now a park maintained by the City of Lookout Mountain.

Said to have been carried to Chattanooga on a train with a passenger traveling from Cuba via New Orleans, the yellow fever epidemic swept through the city with a Memphis traveler. Before it was over, the population had dwindled to 1,800 people, reduced by 366 who died and thousands who fled from the ravages of the withering disease.

An early developer of the area was Major McCullough, known for his yearly caravan of oxcarts, animals, people and a piano as he led his family up Lookout Mountain to the cooler climate of his home by the Natural Bridge. He later established the McCullough Hotel, which would become the Natural Bridge Hotel.

McCullough's ten children—eight of them daughters—would later help build a silk mill and the Flintstone United Methodist Church, a unique stone building once commemorated for its ironic history in *Ripley's Believe It or Not*.

Higher Education

The education of their children was important to those early Chattanoogans, many of whom employed schoolmasters, hosting private schools in their homes. The Prussian-born Professor H.W. Von Alderhoff, the leading schoolmaster of the mid-nineteenth century, was courted by leading citizens to come to Chattanooga to teach in 1850.

Established in 1859 on Lookout Mountain, his Alderhoff Institute for Boys was considered one of the finest educational institutions in the South before the Civil War began in 1861. Renowned for speaking nine languages, the schoolmaster was entrusted with the children of some of the city's most notable families, including the Cravenes, the Whitesides and the Keys. When word came that war had begun at Fort Sumter, the children lit two barrels of coal tar on fire, danced and gave patriotic secessionist speeches. After many of his students went off to fight, Alderhoff closed the school, moving his own family from the mountain back down to Chattanooga for their safety.

In 1866, a year after the war ended, the Lookout Mountain Educational Institute was opened near the Natural Bridge in response to the absence of a public school system.

New York business mogul Christopher R. Robert, founder of Robert College in Constantinople, was devoted to the furtherance of education in the postwar era; his stewardship of the institute allowed him to spread

Students from the Lookout Mountain Institute are pictured here, posing on Sunset Rock during the school's last days before the Civil War's ravages closed its doors.

his educational mission. The Lookout Mountain Educational Institute operated until the Tennessee legislature mandated local management of schools in 1872.

Spiritualists and Oddfellows

The Natural Bridge area also became a haunt for those interested in the netherworld. In 1883, the Southern Spiritualists Association was organized in Chattanooga at a meeting of more than one hundred leaders in the national sect. They leased the Lookout Mountain Hotel, purchased the Natural Bridge Hotel and, as their ranks grew, built larger meeting facilities to accommodate growing numbers at séances, lectures, spirit contacts, feats of extrasensory perception and eerie moonlit meetings featuring war dances among the sandstone sentries. One spiritualist, a Mrs. Cora Glading, spent hours writing, the lines of channeled text moving up from the bottom of the page and readable only with a mirror.

Many of Chattanooga's citizens shared the spiritualists' credo of the "promulgation of the fundamental doctrines of eternal existence and the inter-relation of the Material and Spiritual places of life," according to John Wilson's *Chattanooga's Story*. Possibly responding to the massive death and loss

Formerly known as the Lookout Mountain Hotel, this magnificent building is now home to Covenant College and is the only of the original mountain hotels that remains.

wrought by the Civil War, believers came from all over the country to hear renowned mediums in a setting steeped in ancient auras.

The decision to purchase a Lookout Mountain site for this strange religious sect was made at the Odd Fellows Hall, the home of a benevolent social society from which the spiritualists drew many of their leaders. The moniker "Odd Fellows" was reputed to have been earned in the 1780s when the idea of working-class men working together for a social good was considered peculiar, or odd. Such was the benevolent and social spirit of Chattanooga's Odd Fellows, who manifested the generous principles and practices of the fraternity in their relationships with one another and with the city.

The Hill City and Hamilton Chapters of the Independent Order of Odd Fellows still exist today, one an innocuous door on Frazier Avenue, its windows offering a view of the mountain that has loomed large in its city's history.

There were many Odd Fellows among the ex–Civil War soldiers who attended the 1881 reunion at the Chickamauga Battlefield and celebrated efforts to create both the national cemetery and the first national park. The spirit of the event was reflected in the words of General John T. Wilder, the former Union army leader who returned to Chattanooga and later served as its mayor: "Chattanooga is not a Southern city, not a Northern city…one's politics, religion or section is not called into question here. This is the freest town on the map. All join together here for the general good and strive, to a man, for the upbuilding of the city."

All these former soldiers—Confederate and Union alike—knew they must build their city together if any of them were to prosper in a land ravaged by war. Today, the landscape and names are different, but the passion for the city and its schools is as powerful and the change as real.

RUBY FALLS

Rachel was only twelve years old in 1779, when her family traveled the Tennessee River through what was to become Chattanooga. She likely heard the screams of fellow travelers ambushed and massacred by followers of Chief Dragging Canoe, the Cherokee leader who fought for the British in the Revolutionary War.

Chattanooga has served many times as the intersection of famous people and famous events. Little did the young Rachel know that she would someday become the wife of Andrew Jackson, general and twice president of the United States. We know that "Old Hickory" traveled through Chattanooga as well, and that knowledge has led to one of our area's deepest mysteries: did Old Hickory sign his name on the walls of a cave deep inside Lookout Mountain?

Signature in the Soot

Inhabitants of this area have known of those deep, winding caves for hundreds of years. The underground passages below Ruby Falls were long used by Native Americans. Later, soldiers from both sides of the Civil War used the caves for respite, hospital care and entertainment. Hundreds of Civil War soldiers signed their names in the soot on the walls. The most intriguing signature on the walls, however, is the name any American would recognize: Andrew Jackson. But was Old Hickory himself behind the underground graffiti?

As with many mysteries, we may never really know. Ruby Falls representative Hu Longmire says the famous graffiti likely dates from was 1833, and records from President Andrew Jackson's archives suggest he was not here at that time but was, in fact, touring the Northeast.

Here's what we know for sure: Andrew Jackson was in the area around Chattanooga many times, and he left his mark on the land and the people in many ways.

Jackson and the Cherokee

It was to our south, at the Battle at Horseshoe Bend, Alabama, that in 1814 Cherokees fought for and not against white settlers, under the command of General Jackson and the great Cherokee leader Major Ridge. Jackson and Ridge met again in 1816 at the great council at Turkeytown (near Center, Alabama), where Jackson introduced Cyrus Kingsbury to the Cherokee. Kingsbury, who was on the American Board of Commissioners for Foreign Missions, was instrumental in founding the Brainerd Mission, near what is now Eastgate mall. The mission and school served to educate and Christianize the native Cherokee.

The site of the Brainerd Mission is also the burial site of missionary Samuel Austin Worcester, a friend and supporter of the Cherokee. As treaties came and went, Worcester realized the written word would be the Cherokees' best defense against white settlers anxious to expand their landholdings into Cherokee territory. Along with the famous warrior Sequoyah, who created the Cherokee alphabet, Worcester and Elias Boudinot published the native-language *Cherokee Phoenix* in 1828.

Andrew Jackson became president of the United States the next year, and it was as president that he and Samuel Worcester crossed paths. When Georgia tried to prohibit Worcester from living in the Cherokee region, the Supreme Court, under Chief Justice John Marshall, ruled against the state. Georgia ignored the ruling, as did Andrew Jackson, who is said to have replied, "John Marshall has made his decision, let him enforce it."

From Turkeytown to the Trail of Tears

President Jackson was near the end of his second term in 1836, when Major Ridge and his nephew, Elias Boudinot, signed the Treaty of New Echota, which began the removal of the Cherokee from their ancestral land. Ridge and Boudinot were later executed by the Cherokee for their part in that removal—now known as the Trail of Tears and commemorated in Chattanooga's beautiful waterfront feature, *The Passage*.

Maybe someday a clever investigator can determine for sure whether the president walked the hidden passages deep below Ruby Falls and whether it is, indeed, his signature on the ancient cave walls. But one thing we know for sure: Andrew Jackson, the Cherokee and Chattanooga were bound by history, and Andrew Jackson left a lasting mark on the history of our area.

Investigators Still Exploring New Worlds in Chattanooga

Today, Ruby Falls is a dazzling display of rock formations and is an exciting part of the attractions available on Lookout Mountain. Still curious about that signature in the caves below the falls, I found some true-blue cavers whose

The waterfall inside the Ruby Falls Caverns is 150 feet tall and was named for its founder's wife, Ruby Lambert.

eyes gleamed as they talked about the "nirvana" that was the underground cave they visited in 1992. They saw the Andrew Jackson signature and then ventured farther into depths that few have reached. There they found a bear skull and the jawbone of a large cat, and they even took a plaster cast of an animal's footprint.

Imagine being one of the first humans to see an underground world! There is still plenty for investigators to discover in Chattanooga, where the outdoors hold adventures for everyone.

How to Make a Mountain

Lookout Mountain is mostly made from limestone. Imagine that 240 million years ago, a shallow sea covered the eastern Tennessee area, home to what would become Lookout Mountain. Here's how that sea created our most visible landmark, according to rubyfalls.com:

> *Limestone is a rock formed by successive layers or shale, sand, and pebbly sand. The layers of sediment hardened over time to form limestone rock. Millions of years ago the North American and African plates collided in a collision that lasted for several thousand years. The collision was felt even as far inland as the Chattanooga area. These tectonic forces produced a series of earthquakes that pushed and bent the hardened rock to form mountains.*

Thousands of visitors visit Ruby Falls every year with its spectacular underground waterfall. Few of them realize that there are more treasures beneath their feet!

SUNSET ROCK

The view from Sunset Rock is miraculous, the vista spreading out before the eyes a wonderful testament to the work of nature. As surely as there will be paths toward clean water, there will always be a path to a place so beautiful, and in that beauty man will find inspiration.

Moccasin Bend and Williams Island below represent one of the largest contiguous archaeological excavations of life in the Tennessee Valley, dating back at least fourteen thousand years, and it is reasonable to assume that the trail to Sunset Rock has memories that are as old.

Union and Confederate generals vied for control of Chattanooga, its railroads and its strategic views. Civil War generals and sightseeing soldiers often left the valley with pictures from Sunset Rock.

Civil War generals, celebrities, tourists, families and even the King of Prussia have been photographed on the amazing outcropping, their figures silhouettes against the magnificent vista of seven states.

CHESTNUT BLIGHT

In the early years of the 1900s, the landscape of southern Appalachia and the Cumberland Plateau began to look like the sort of bleak horror that families today remember from photographs of the damage from Hurricane Katrina. But the first things to fall were not homes, but massive trees—some of them over one hundred feet tall, with trunks ten feet in diameter. And the natural disaster wasn't a storm but a mysterious blight that raged through our region, decimating the American chestnut and many of the societies supported by the chestnut culture.

Enormous Impact

While it took two men to wrap their arms around an American chestnut, the majestic tree's girth paled in comparison to its economic impact. To understand the impact that the trees, their nuts and symbiotic undergrowth once made on the southeastern United States, we can look to the Mediterranean island of Corsica, which has used the chestnut tree from root to fruit since the thirteenth century. Some chestnuts in Corsica's wild-growth areas are said to stand a staggering 1,600 feet tall, and the gargantuan trees are woven into the very core of Corsican culture, providing food, wine, beer, flour, building materials and the economic base upon which the island continues to thrive.

The American chestnut stood tall, creating a canopy of sustainability that spread up the eastern coast, the goods harvested from it providing for the poor in the Appalachian Valley.

The American chestnut (*Castanea dentate*) was once a keystone species in our forest; Appalachian lore holds that a squirrel could travel the chestnut canopy from Georgia to Maine, always fed and never touching the ground. It was also one of the most important trees in the southern Appalachian Mountains, anchoring not only the forest ecosystem but also the economy of nearby communities.

When nearly four billion American chestnuts on over 220 million acres succumbed to the blight, the entire culture of the region began to change. In an already dirt-poor region, the nuts fed families and livestock and were even used as currency. The wood, meanwhile, was an opportunity to build a home and export a product. Together, the loss of nuts and wood was a devastation from which communities did not recover; for many, it made the difference between subsistence and starvation. The early 1910s echoed with the sounds of the mighty trees falling victim to the blight. Now, with the famous tree still teetering on the brink of extinction, many of the towns, hollows and homes of the Appalachian region are only distant memories to the oldest members of the population.

Mystery of the Blight

The mystery of the origin of the blight remains unanswered. Research suggests the fungus was accidentally introduced when Asian chestnut trees infected with the virus but immune to its ravages were brought to North America. A prevailing historical rumor suggested that Americans infected the Japanese tree population in the early 1900s. While that first example of biological subterfuge is likely fiction, the lessons of the blight continue to serve as a vivid reminder that our natural world is a fragile system and should be protected.

In the Chattanooga valley, the American chestnut was part of the landscape and lore well before written records exist. The ancient Cherokee called it the "bread tree," just like the Corsicans. These cultures, worlds apart, savored the sweet meat of the chestnut and the society supported under its broad canopy. A hub of rail traffic, Chattanooga saw more than its share of chestnut-based commerce as the timber flowed through its valley to help build railroads, furnish homes and feed the hunger for the iconic roasted chestnut treat.

Lookout Mountain

Conservation—and a Discovery

As in much of the Southeast, this growth and industry took its toll in Chattanooga; by mid-century, ecology, nature and air quality had become victims of clear-cut timber harvesting, garbage dumping and rampant pollution. Fortunately, Chattanooga was home to a man who quietly set about to save the land that had provided for his ancestors in order to conserve it for his descendants. Robert M. Davenport began acquiring land in 1958. Upon his death in 1994, he passed to his family both the land and his passion for the conservation. The Lula Lake Land Trust was born, a dream conceived of and nurtured by a man whose legacy may allow future generations to learn from past mistakes, to care for their world and to embrace the beauty of the land entrusted them.

William G. Raoul, another man with deep Chattanooga roots, shared Robert Davenport's passion for conservation. The longtime member of the American Chestnut Foundation was passionate about preserving part of our region's history and supporting research to save the majestic tree from extinction. His exuberance and dedication led to local chestnut plantations at the Lula Lake Land Trust, Bendabout Farm and Reflection Riding and the birth of the Chattanooga Chestnut Tree Project.

The living laboratory gained life in the early 1980s, when William Raoul's Lookout Mountain neighbor, Bill Crutchfield, felt the familiar prick of a chestnut burr. Crutchfield was hiking near the west end of Eagle's Bluff on Lookout Mountain, overlooking the valley that his family already had called home for generations, when the chestnut blight raged.

He shared the news with the spry octogenarian William G. Raoul, who scrambled up the cliff to find two flowering American chestnut trees. Imagine how his eyes must have glowed—the lifelong champion of the chestnut, discovering those trees.

Today, students at UTC can learn from the equally powerful enthusiasm of Hill Craddock, a professor leading the charge to save the American chestnut. And Chattanoogans can visit the Lula Lake Land Trust to see the American chestnut in what was once a horizon that its canopy defined.

LULA LAKE LAND TRUST

Created in 1994, the Lula Lake Land Trust began with the gift of history, a legacy of the lake and the falls and the 770 acres that surround them. The land trust has now directly protected more than 7,800 acres, beginning with the 40,000-acre Rock Creek watershed. Its partnership with the Cloudland Canyon State Park leverages federal funds to increase the umbrella of protection and creates an unbroken conservation landscape more than twenty miles long.

Cloudland Canyon

The "Cloudland Connector" trail project will offer a multiuse trail connecting the huge landscape to the people who live and work around it, offering a unique experience to appreciate the wonder and bounty of nature in the Tennessee Valley.

Reflection Riding

Can the spirit of a man change the face of a mountain?

Science says that the elements change rocks. But maybe if we take a cue from the Native Americans, with their love of the land, we can see what a great chief saw centuries ago: his own face, carved from rock, 1,200 feet above his beloved valley.

> *In the old days, a great Indian chief lay dying in Lookout Valley. He was the last member of a once powerful tribe. He regretted that there was no one to mourn his death and know that he had lived. He prayed to his gods for a sign that he and his tribe should not perish utterly, but be remembered in days to come.*
>
> *As he prayed, a great storm swept up the valley, shaking the mountain and throwing down huge rocks. The next day the dying chief saw on the side of the mountain his own likeness carved from rock. He died content, knowing that he would not be forgotten as long as his image looked out over the valley.*

During the time of the Cherokee, that formation was called "Father Rock," and offerings were made at its base to honor the old. Later, white men and soldiers called it "Sunset Rock," and settlers and sightseers took pictures from it and posed happily on it, taking no notice of the majestic profile under them.

Lookout Mountain

Now that famous rock face overlooks Reflection Riding and the Chattanooga Nature Center. They exist together alongside the winding Lookout Creek, home to dazzling displays of native wildflowers, field flowers, ferns, shrubs and trees, as well as a significant collection of endangered animals.

The beauty of this land makes it hard to imagine the bloodshed that marked its history.

Beauty's Bloody History

Chief Dragging Canoe moved his people to this area after telling the white man, "You have bought a fair land but will find its settlement dark and bloody." That bloodshed continued as he and fellow warriors from the Cherokee's "Five Lower Towns" fought on the side of the British in the last battle of the Revolutionary War in 1782.

During the Civil War, this site again echoed with the sounds of war. On a foggy November morning in 1863, Union soldiers crossed Lookout Creek and climbed the west side of the mountain to where Confederate forces waited at Point Lookout. The famous fight to follow would later be called the "Battle above the Clouds."

The Chambliss family, with the generosity typical of Chattanoogans, played a major part in changing the face of this western side of the mountain. In 1895, when a private enterprise threatened to keep visitors from the point, Adolph Ochs and Alexander Chambliss, who had both adopted Chattanooga as home, worked to ensure that the federal government purchased much of the western slope as part of the National Military Park.

Rescuing History's Sacred Spots

During the mid-1900s, this land was again threatened, though this time by industrialization. In 1956, another Chambliss came to the rescue of the nature and spirit of the land his father had defended. John and Margaret Chambliss created a place for reflection, home to the breathtaking flowers that bloomed for the legendary Indian chief and soldiers of the Revolutionary and Civil Wars.

Today, peace is the order of the day, and many Chattanooga families continue to work to preserve the spirit of quiet reflection in this once embattled land. Trails reach up the mountain to join those of the National Park Service, and hikers can imagine that they are following the steps of generations of warriors while enjoying the natural beauty.

Natural elements carved the planes of the face on the mountain, but Chattanoogans worked to preserve the beauty that surrounds it. We continue to honor the spirit of the land that allows us all to appreciate it.

Reflection Riding Arboretum & Botanical Garden
400 Garden Road
(423) 821-9582
www.reflectionriding.org

RACCOON MOUNTAIN

Hernando de Soto explored the Southeast in search of gold as early as 1540, and the 1828 discovery that precipitated the country's first gold rush in Dahlonega, Georgia, was old news to the region's Cherokee inhabitants. Major Ridge, a powerful Cherokee leader and statesman, is often described as having been adorned in gold and wearing robes edged with gold.

The 1828 discovery of gold in our area hastened the removal of the Cherokee; the first land grants, issued in 1839 to James A. Whiteside and F.W. Lea, were inked as the Cherokees' soft steps away from their homes still echoed in the hills of the Cumberland Plateau. In their wake, pioneers and settlers streamed into the Chattanooga valley, grasping at land grants and eager to till the fertile Tennessee soil. Whispers of hidden Cherokee treasure spread as the newcomers imagined hordes of the precious gold hidden in the caves honeycombing the nearby mountains.

But treasure wasn't the only thing waiting for them there.

Creepy Caverns

In 1914, a contributor to the *Chattanooga Times* wrote about the adventures of one would-be gold digger, a man he called "Bolt." (You'll soon know why.) Bolt had attended a séance during which, he said, he was visited by the spirit of a departed friend. The friend revealed to Bolt the location of a cave near Chattanooga with a cache of silver that would lead to fabulous wealth.

Armed with a chart rendered from the minute descriptions provided by the "spirit," a team of men made their way through the wild woods of Raccoon Mountain—though they had to struggle to overcome the strange behavior of their horses, which seemed spooked as the team drew near the mysterious cave entrance.

Lashed together, the men descended into the gloomy depths of the cave. As they traversed the narrow passages, they marveled at the pictures of animals on the walls, the man-made anterooms or sleeping quarters and the arrowheads that littered the floors of caves that were clearly well used. According to the *Times*, they also heard unexplained noises and experienced eerie sensations that sent them running: "Neither of the men could fully explain it but they seemed to be joined by an invisible something or somebody…they literally flew out of the small entrance and dashed madly toward the mouth of the cave."

Led by their otherworldly guide to the hidden cave entrance, these treasure hunters tried time and again to penetrate the maze of passageways under Raccoon Mountain, boldly searching for the treasures of legendary chieftains and robbers but daunted by the mysterious occurrences that befell each attempt. Written seventy-five years after the Cherokee left their land, the *Times* account makes it easy to imagine that these treasure seekers battled the specter of those angry spirits in those caves, some populated by a peculiar species of blind fish living in a rapid-flowing stream of unknown depth.

Echoes of More Recent Past

Another sixty years later, those same Raccoon Mountain caverns echoed with different sounds as 1,600 workers and their machinery removed 546,400 cubic yards of rock to hollow out a massive tunnel in the Bangor limestone.

What we now know as TVA's Raccoon Mountain Pumped Storage Plant is capable of producing enough electricity for 800,000 homes. When the TVA system needs added power, water is pumped from the Tennessee River to a reservoir on Raccoon Mountain and then released into the limestone funnel beneath. The 528-acre reservoir can be filled in twenty-seven hours and is 142 feet deep. When full, the reservoir is one of the biggest lakes in southeast Tennessee. When empty, it's the Grand Canyon of Tennessee.

Heralded by the National Society of Civil Engineers as a top engineering feat, the Raccoon Mountain facility can generate up to 1,570 megawatts of electricity for up to twenty continuous hours during peak demand times, as water from the upper lake falls through fifteen-foot-diameter turbines at a rate of three thousand cubic feet of water per second and is finally discharged into Nickajack Lake. It would take fourteen Chickamauga Dams to produce the same amount of power produced by this fascinating plant.

Raccoon Mountain is a fascinating pumped-water storage unit, providing electricity through its magnificent turbines. It is also home to thousands of acres of paths and trails for today's Chattanoogans.

Mountain Still Thrills

Just west of Chattanooga, Raccoon Mountain is only six miles from downtown, yet its three thousand acres are certified by the Wildlife Habitat Council and are home to ball fields, picnic areas, playgrounds and walking trails. Visitors can see an array of flora and fauna indigenous to the region, including hawks whose spirals in the sky sometimes seem to mirror the whirlpool-like action of the massive funnel in the mountain.

At the visitors' center, guests can learn more about the mountain, the lake and the storage plant's massive, 382.5-megawatt generators. But for sheer excitement, few things can match the thirty-eight-level elevator ride that drops 30 feet per second for an agonizing fifty-two seconds, as the car races down into a 490-foot-long, 72-foot-wide chamber deep into a mountain that still holds secrets, power and promise.

Chapter 4
FROM THE CITICO MOUND
TO THE VOLKSWAGEN PLANT

CITICO MOUND

He was searching for the "burn," that legendary feeling runners yearn for, but found bones instead.

Dr. Nick Honerkamp is a legend in Chattanooga for many reasons, chief among them his role as acting head of the Sociology, Geology and Anthropology Department of the University of Tennessee at Chattanooga. In this role, he is the go-to man for questions regarding bones and their history in this area. In a remarkable twist of fate, it was he who, in 2002, discovered some really amazing bones.

Dr. Honerkamp is also an avid proponent of running and was jogging on Amnicola Highway near the site of the Water Company complex in 2002 when his practiced eye caught the outline of human bones in the jagged earth along the river's edge.

Restaurant owner Lawton Haygood (the Boathouse, Canyon Grill, Sugar's) paused construction of the Boathouse, formerly the site of the Sandbar Restaurant, when the bones were discovered. State law mandates that officials have five working days to determine the significance of all human remains discovered in Tennessee.

Felonious Fill Dirt

The Citico Mound was a prominent landmark seen by Chattanoogans above the great bend of the Tennessee River since before our recorded history. The

The Citico Mound represented thousands of years of life on the Tennessee River and was located near the Tennessee American Water Company facility and the Boathouse Restaurant.

top of the mound must have seemed to touch the sky compared to the flat line of its surrounding horizon. In 1930, this mound was described by a report to the Smithsonian Institution as having been composed of alternate layers of earth and ashes, being raised only 2 or 3 feet at a time to a total height of 19 feet. The imposing mound was oval shaped and was 158 feet long by 128 feet wide at the base, and its flat top was 82 feet long by 44 feet wide and was estimated to have taken over one hundred years to construct. Imagine such an impressive structure built well before the first European face saw this land.

Another mound, some thirty feet in height and perhaps one hundred feet in diameter, was the "lookout" station for Chief Citico and was near Caney Creek. Other ancient dwelling sites in this area included "six within the present city limits on Chattanooga Creek, seven on the south bank of the Tennessee River, five on the north bank, three on Maclellan Island, five on Williams Island," according to James W. Livingood's book *The Chattanooga Country*, and the Moccasin Bend area was "almost a continuous site."

The site was explored during the Civil War by Federal soldiers who used it as a recreational garden area and studied by representatives from the Smithsonian in 1865, by a party from the Academy of Natural Sciences of Philadelphia in 1915 and by Chattanoogans during and since. It was owned for five generations by the Gardenhire family.

Amnicola Highway was once called Dixie Highway, and much of the mound was used to grade that new roadway. Again, in 1957, the mound and its significant contents were used as fill dirt for the expansion of Amnicola Highway.

The Corn that Cracked the Case

The who, the what and, most of all, the when of our earliest settlers are questions that have occupied the thoughts of citizens and scientists in the Chattanooga area. While Native American representatives prefer that the remains are left where they are found, many archaeologists, anthropologists and scientists feel that not exhuming and exploring the area of ancient grave sites does history a disservice. There is not a state law to mandate the handling of such remains, but time is allowed for the medical examiner's office to determine that the remains are not of significant forensic value. For every expert who has studied the Citico Mound and the hundreds of graves interred around it, there may be another date put forward to identify Chattanooga's earliest residents.

Science seems to most to be, well, not so exact; however, advances are such that the techniques considered cutting-edge in 1930 look prehistoric compared to the radiocarbon dating and isotope studies available to today's scientific investigators. Dr. Honerkamp and Tom Bodkin, a forensic anthropologist with the medical examiner's office, used radiocarbon dating to determine that the bones found along the river were from a period between 790 BC and 420 BC, or were between 2,427 and 2,797 years old.

The radiocarbon dating supplemented and confirmed what the other methods used had suggested. Scientists use isotope studies to examine the diet of the deceased to glean more information about their lives and the time in which they lived. The people discovered by the river here had a terrestrial diet as opposed to a strictly marine diet.

The presence, or lack thereof, of corn was an important factor in dating these particular bones, as corn was not introduced to North America until between the years 1100 and 1400, over nine hundred years ago. Writing for the Tennessee Anthropological Association newsletter,

Dr. Honerkamp remarked that this site was a "ceremonial and village center…and exists now only as small buried remnants. The tragic history of neglect, indifference and willful destruction at this site constitutes a sad and enduring legacy for Chattanooga."

TENNESSEE RIVERWALK

A twenty-mile trail system, the Tennessee Riverwalk connects Ross's Landing with the Chickamauga Dam via a beautiful path along the river, allowing people to connect fun, fitness and nature. Signs depicting the blue ribbon of the Tennessee River amid the green of the valley dot the road alongside Amnicola Highway, guiding travelers to the many stops offering boat portals, restrooms and parking for Chattanooga's cyclists, runners and walkers.

TENNESSEE RIVER RAILROAD BRIDGE/CINCINNATI SOUTHERN RAILWAY BRIDGE, CHICKAMAUGA DAM AND CHICKAMAUGA LAKE

Can you imagine climbing up and down a ladder with 120 steps—five times a week? Or spending the whole day in a 576-square-foot, tin-sided house—170 feet above a surging river and atop a much-used bridge?

That once was daily life for the man in charge of the Tenbridge, the railroad bridge just downstream from the Chickamauga Dam. Originally built in 1888, portions of it burned in 1914, and it was completely rebuilt in 1920. The bridge was staffed full time with a watchman, or bridge tender, until the early 1970s. The bridge tender's office was the "house in the sky" you've probably gazed up at while driving along Access Road. Now imagine the many people who must have made that daily vertical commute during the eighty-two years the house was manned. Some of those bridge tenders stood watch as the Chickamauga Dam was being built in 1936.

They saw the Tennessee Valley change as the power of TVA began to manage "forests and rivers as integrated systems rather than isolated resources," according to Gifford Pinchot's writings on www.tva.com. Prior to TVA's changes in the landscape, the valley was suffering from the effects of erosion and poor land management. Conservation efforts must have dramatically changed the view from that tall, tall house.

This house sits atop a vertical list truss bridge 170 feet above the Tennessee River. Until the 1970s, the house was manned daily, the watchman climbing 120 steps to his post.

Tending the Tenbridge

Chattanooga children have probably created thousands of chilling and fantastic stories about that house during the 118 years that one has been there. Did you? Do your children?

After some investigating, I found the granddaughter of a man who spent much of his career atop that busy bridge. Linda Roberts, a teacher at the Northside Learning Center, has spent a career teaching and tending to classrooms of eager young minds. Her grandfather was Andler Wesley Rhea, but she knew him as "Patchee." When I wondered aloud at what a courageous man he must have been to climb that ladder every day, she laughed. He was the father of nine children, she said; it's likely that climbing that ladder wasn't the hardest thing he did in an average day!

Favorite of the "Railfans"

The house in the sky, a Chattanooga landmark, guards one of the two bridges of interest in Tennessee to a large community of railroad enthusiasts. The Tenbridge (or Tennessee River Railroad Bridge) is 1,800 feet long and is a truss bridge with a vertical lift. That means that the center portion of the bridge can be raised to allow for boats with tall masts or large barges to pass under it. That's only happened a handful of times since the 1980s, but the massive reels and motors that control the lift are housed in that unusual building.

Wikipedia, the online encyclopedia, lists this historic Chattanooga landmark among its directory of unique railroad sites. The Tenbridge has long fascinated railway enthusiasts, or "railfans." Among them was Dr. James W. Livingood, an iconic figure in the study of Chattanooga history. He believed that all roads cross in Chattanooga, and he attributed this to the importance of rivers and railroads for transportation of people and goods early in the city's history. His eyes sparkled when he talked about Chattanooga and the rail system, and that same sparkle is evident in the photographs on websites dedicated to rail enthusiasts and their historic hobby.

In a time when few people travel the rail lines of America there exists a vibrant culture of people like Dr. Livingood, who appreciates the wonder of the railways, trains and bridges. For railfans across the country, as for Chattanooga's children (and former children), the "house in the sky" has long been a unique and awesome sight.

Fast facts: Tennessee River and TVA
The Tennessee River is 650 miles long.
The river is the largest tributary of the Ohio River.
The Tennessee Valley Authority, which built the Chickamauga Dam by the Tenbridge, was founded in 1933.
The Chickamauga Lake displaced nine hundred families, has three cities submerged under its 35,400 acres and was purchased as a part of a 60,000-acre purchase.

ENGEL STADIUM

Since its earliest days, Chattanooga has drawn unique people. Explorers, missionaries, soldiers, innovators, adventurers, builders and artists have

Engel Stadium was revolutionary when Joe Engel, the Barnum of Baseball, bought the Chattanooga Lookouts. Babe Ruth was struck out by a girl in an exposition game here with the New York Yankees.

come here with their dreams to the lush valley where the mountains face one another. Rush Montgomery, one of Chattanooga's pioneering citizens, once described this place as "the funnel of the world."

In the world of sports, the Scenic City witnessed a confluence of events that would resonate through the women's movement and baseball history, and they all took place in a stadium that embodied the spirit of its founder and of Chattanooga itself.

The Barnum of Baseball

As Americans celebrated the turn of the twentieth century, the country caught baseball fever. The iconic American sport expanded, with Major League teams sponsoring minor league franchises. Baseball continued to buoy the national spirit even as the Depression cut a swath of despair and poverty through the country.

In 1929, the owner of the Washington Senators, a Major League power, sent a young scout named Joe Engel down south to acquire a minor league team. Cash in hand, Engel went to Atlanta to buy that city's farm league team, the Crackers. But the lure of Chattanooga drew him here instead. Leaving the Atlanta Crackers in the dust, Engel purchased the Chattanooga Lookouts and agreed to build a fine new facility at East Third and O'Neal Streets.

The son of a German immigrant, Engel had been a batboy and then team mascot for the Senators. Later, he pitched for the team. With an earned run average of 3.34, he contributed to the single-game record for the most batters hit by a pitch.

What he lacked in prowess, however, he made up for in gusto. His new stadium in Chattanooga was ready in the nick of time for the start of the 1930 baseball season, and the sports world was already abuzz with the news of one of the first press boxes, a raised hill at center field and one of the deepest center fields in the country, measuring 471 feet from home plate.

Engel was also ready for the national attention. The natural showman quickly earned the affectionate nicknames the "Baron of Ballyhoo" and the "Barnum of Baseball," orchestrating elaborate stunts to attract and entertain

Joe Engel, the Barnum of Baseball, was very proud of his ladies' team, the Englettes. He is pictured here with his star player, Jackie Mitchell.

people and keep them coming back. Engel stationed a barber's chair in the bleachers, offering a shave and a haircut to Lookouts fans. Once, as the Great Depression still raged, he raffled off a house, packing twenty-four thousand people into the twelve-thousand-capacity stadium and breaking a record for attendance at a game.

In 1931, Engel orchestrated the now famous exhibition game between the Chattanooga Lookouts and the New York Yankees, featuring his secret weapon: a seventeen-year-old female pitcher named Jackie Mitchell. In seven pitches, she struck out both Lou Gehrig and the infamous Sultan of Swat, Babe Ruth. When media backlash resulted in Mitchell's contract being voided by the commissioner of baseball, Engel created an all-girls' team, the Engelettes, in support of women and their right to play.

Jackie Mitchell, the young lady who struck out the great Babe Ruth, later visited the historic Engel Stadium to sign autographs for a cheering crowd.

New Life for Engel

Although the Lookouts left Engel Stadium in 1999, it is still considered one of the top minor league parks in the country, and it has witnessed decades of landmark events in baseball history. There have been outlandish stunts, like the fake safaris in which Joe Engel paraded papier-mâché elephants before the crowd; the pregame show that Engel broadcast from atop exotic animals; and the camels that a later owner brought onto that notorious center field.

But there also has been a veritable hall of fame at Engel. Names like Michael Jordan, Babe Ruth, Lou Gehrig, Billy Graham, Willie Mays, Satchel Paige and Harmon Killebrew will be forever attached to the stadium and its spirit.

In Chattanooga fashion, the historic Engel Stadium has been given new life, invigorated by its inclusion on the National Registry of Historic Places and its acquisition by the University of Tennessee at Chattanooga. Soon, the nearby Fortwood community will resonate with the sounds of music and community spirit and life again as Engel Stadium supports the students and community of UTC and Chattanooga.

CITIZEN'S CEMETERY

William Gardenhire was the grandson of a German immigrant. Married to a Cherokee, he was able to own property prior to the Removal Act, and he and his family had a large farm near the Tennessee River and the Citico Mound, where he operated a ferry. Much of that property is occupied by cemeteries with historic roots to the earliest Chattanoogans. The Citizen's Cemetery, the Confederate Cemetery and the Jewish Cemetery trace their residents to the first families of Chattanooga, though ad hoc war burials and the removal of headstones during the Union's fervor to build fortifications make accurate records difficult. Headstones that survived the Union thefts included names like Crutchfield, Reese Brabson and John P. Long.

Bordered by Third Street, Fifth Street and Collins and Douglas Streets, the shade from its massive trees makes the area a historic setting for a modern-day picnic across from the bustling Chattanooga School for the Arts and Sciences and down the street from the modern Baroness Erlanger Medical Center.

BARONESS ERLANGER MEDICAL CENTER

Members of European royalty were frequent visitors to Chattanooga, enjoying the city and the social events surrounding the growth of the region. The Baron Emile d'Erlanger was a chief railroad official married to the daughter of a prominent member of the Confederate government. The wealthy baron was courted by city leaders and members of the medical profession to support the building of the city's first hospital. Named for his wife, the Baroness Erlanger, the laying of the cornerstone was celebrated in 1891 at the Harrison Avenue (now East Third Street) location of the four-acre site. Though it wasn't opened until 1899, its service to the Chattanooga community was critical during the city's growth and continues, now including the T.C. Thompson's Children's Hospital, a destination for families seeking the best in medical attention.

ORCHARD KNOB

The Orchard Knob Reservation is officially part of the Chickamauga and Chattanooga National Military Park. On November 23, 1863, Union general U.S. Grant moved a substantial portion of his army forward from his lines in Chattanooga toward Missionary Ridge. After a brief fight, the Federals swept Confederate resistance aside and captured this little hill halfway there. Two days later, Orchard Knob became Grant's vantage point for viewing the dramatic victory on Missionary Ridge. Monuments, cannons and signs can be found on the hill with a dramatic Union viewpoint of Missionary Ridge.

NATIONAL CEMETERY

"My train was captured this a.m. at Big Shanty, evidently by Federal soldiers in disguise. They are making rapidly for Chattanooga, possibly with the idea of burning the railroad bridges in their rear. If I do not capture them in the meantime, see that they do not pass Chattanooga."

Imagine a world where communication was limited to telegrams, letters and personal conversations—where, faced with a crisis, you had to tap out a telegraph message instead of dialing a phone or texting.

William Fuller was the conductor of the General, a train running between Atlanta and Chattanooga during the Civil War. While eating breakfast in

Kennesaw, Georgia, he saw his train moving away, hijacked by the enemy and apparently bent on destruction. His telegraphed message alerted troops and civilians that a drama was being played out in their backyard, word that sent Chattanooga into a state of panic and chaos.

The Great Locomotive Chase

In 1862, a team of twenty-two Union spies disguised as civilians infiltrated Chattanooga. They stayed at the Crutchfield House (now the site of the Read House) and toured our city. It was a critical time during the Civil War, and Chattanooga was a vital part of the Union strategy for success. Control of the Western and Atlantic Railway meant power over communications and the movements of troops and munitions.

The leader of the raiding party was James Andrews, an experienced Federal spy who gained the trust of citizens and Confederate soldiers to gather information. Andrews had tried before to disrupt the Southern war effort by hijacking a train; according to reports in the *Chattanooga Times*, he vowed he would succeed this time or "leave his bones in Dixie."

Andrews's Raiders captured the train engine, the General, from Big Shanty. A sign near Calhoun, Georgia, commemorates the site.

When Andrews's Raiders took over the General in Kennesaw, Conductor Fuller chased them on foot, then with a handcar and with another train engine. As the Raiders got closer to Chattanooga, the General had a mechanical problem, and the harrowing railway race ended; the Raiders were captured.

Soon, all of Chattanooga was talking about the chase and capture of Andrews's Raiders; the story was printed in both local papers. James Andrews escaped from his jail cell and swam the Tennessee River, naked and cold, until he reached Williams Island—only to be returned to the authorities and hanged in Atlanta.

In all, seven of the Raiders were hanged in Atlanta. They are buried in a circle around a monument to the General near the entrance of Chattanooga's National Cemetery. The rest of the Raiders escaped or were exchanged for Union-held prisoners in 1863; they were the first recipients of the Medal of Honor.

Even Walt Disney was enthralled with the story, which he dramatized in his 1956 movie, *The Great Locomotive Chase.*

Hijacked Again

But for Chattanooga, the saga wasn't over yet.

In 1961 the General disappeared quietly from its home at Union station amid rumors that it was being refurbished for a centennial reenactment. Later, in 1967, Chattanooga's mayor, Ralph Kelley, learned that the train was due to stop in Chattanooga on the way to its new home in Kennesaw, Georgia—the site of its original hijacking.

Mayor Kelley, Hamilton County sheriff Frank Newell, Chattanooga police chief Jack Shasteen and the entire city commission planned another hijacking. As they launched their midnight raid, these proud Chattanoogans were armed with historical facts, a court order and an eye-in-the-sky report from friends Ed and LaVonne Jolley. Newspaper reports detail the hour-by-hour mission to recapture a piece of Chattanooga history.

Mayor Kelley and his team had everything planned. They got a court order and put old police cars on the railroad track in case the train's workers refused to accept the document. All that was left was to catch the General.

That's where an old friendship came into play. Mayor Kelley asked his former University of Chattanooga fraternity brother, pilot Ed Jolley, to help him find the train. Ed and LaVonne Jolley flew so low at times they could hear dogs barking as they searched the rail lines for the train's distinctive colors. Finally, eagle-eye LaVonne Jolley spotted the General's catcher peeking out of a rail barn in Nashville—and the raiding plan fell into place. Chattanooga recaptured the General.

This time, the battle over the General was waged in several courts. Chattanoogans lost their hard-fought bid to keep their historical treasure. But while the General is still on display in Kennesaw, it will always be Chattanooga's Choo-Choo.

Interesting Facts about Chattanooga's Choo-Choo Caper

- Andrews's Raiders were the first recipients of the Medal of Honor.
- The judge who in 1967 ruled against Chattanooga in the city's bid to keep the General was the same judge who convicted labor union leader Jimmy Hoffa of jury tampering.
- Ed Jolley, the pilot who helped locate the General in 1967, is a descendant by marriage of William Fuller, the conductor of the General when it was hijacked a century earlier.

MCCALLIE SCHOOL

Thomas McCallie came to Chattanooga with his wife in 1841 from Rhea County. His grandfather was an immigrant from Scotland who arrived on American shores in 1775. Colonel McCallie ran a faithful home, with his children celebrating family worship in the mornings and evenings. The McCallie family homestead was home to a booming mercantile business and was the site of the first Baylor School. Spencer Jarnagin McCallie and James Park McCallie, sons of the Reverend Thomas Hooke McCallie, were teaching outside of the region when their hopes germinated in the form of the McCallie School, a Chattanooga effort supported by their father. Based at the family farm, a large site at the base of Missionary Ridge, the school opened in 1905 with the promise of wholesome values, a Christian education and healthy standards for its male student body.

Generations of the McCallie family managed the school, growing the campus and the student body until it became recognized as one of the leading private schools in the country. Its boarding halls were home to such legendary graduates as Ted Turner and sons of the leading families in Chattanooga.

MISSIONARY RIDGE

In the early 1800s, the Tennessee Valley was a wilderness frontier, and many of the pioneers traveling by river found a safe harbor on its shores in Chattanooga. When the Trail of Tears left land open for purchase by lottery, the city leaders were already eagerly planning new streets, laying out an expanded version of a city that had been bursting at the seams.

There was just one obstacle to the city's expansion—and it was a big one. The ridges and mountains to the east and south of the city stood in the way of the railroads that promised to open Chattanooga to the world. But even a mountain was no match for a determined southern city. Chattanooga is now known for its strategic and beautiful tunnels. Two railroad tunnels—one through Missionary Ridge and the other linking Chattanooga to Georgia— were both history-making in themselves and the site of some of the city's most dramatic history, including a mission through a mountain, a hijacked train bent on destruction and even the saga of a missing leg.

Overcoming an Obstacle

Two centuries ago, the journey from Ross's Landing (one of Chattanooga's early names) to the Brainerd Mission (where Eastgate Mall and the Brainerd Cemetery now stand) was a perilous trek through heavy, uninhabited woods. In 1828, a hunting party in the area wrote that during their expedition they saw "no sign of a house, cabin or wigwam...not a single human inhabitant except possibly one." It's easy to imagine the "one," traveling solo. Later, the path taken by those early missionaries would come to be known Missionary Ridge.

Even as rail lines were marking fast trade routes across the United States, that near-vertical ridge, five hundred feet high and several miles long, marked the eastern boundary of Chattanooga's geographic and economic reach.

In the 1850s, the Missionary Ridge Railroad Tunnel, one of the earliest railroad tunnels in the South, broke through that barrier. Also called the Whiteside Tunnel and the Chattanooga, Harrison, Georgetown and Charleston Railroad Tunnel, it is a marvel of brick, rock and limestone masonry. The hard-rock tunnel was an engineering landmark, its portals constructed in the shape of a horseshoe. In its sheer rock faces you can still see the lines where the building crew hand-drilled holes, filled them with gunpowder, ignited them and raced away, fleeing the explosion and the flying rock.

Providing the eastern link to the major railway lines into the city, the Missionary Ridge line helped Chattanooga become an important transportation hub. But nature had placed an even more formidable obstacle south of the city.

Breaking through a Barrier

In Chattanooga, the passion for the rail began early; local leaders campaigned for their fledgling city to be the terminus of a railroad to run between the Chattahoochee River in Marthasville, Georgia—a place we now call Atlanta—and the Tennessee River. Chattanoogans celebrated when the Western and Atlantic Railroad laid the first line from Marthasville.

But the enthusiastic city with hardworking boosters came flat up against it in the face of the imposing 1830s' Depression and the rugged north Georgia mountains. Finally, after a decade-long delay, gangs of workmen from both sides tunneled under Chetoogetta Mountain. They met in the middle with a "loud and deafening shout" as sweaty workers armed with picks, axes and determination conquered obstacles to open Chattanooga's rail line.

The tunnel they built, 1,447 feet long, was completed in 1850. The Georgia community that grew up around it was called "Tunnel Hill."

Tunnels, Trains and Turmoil

The strategic importance of the thousands of feet of railroad tunnel at Missionary Ridge and Tunnel Hill brought major changes to Chattanooga's economy. It also played into the battle plans of both sides during the Civil War. Union spies stayed at the Crutchfield House (now the site of the Read House), across from the train depot, while planning a now notorious mission: to hijack a train and, destroying tracks, bridges and tunnels, cut the Confederacy off from its critical supply lines. During what would later be called the Great Railroad Chase, the citizens of Chattanooga rallied when Andrews's Raiders, on their stolen train engine, screamed toward the city, bent on destruction.

In the Chattanooga valley, generals faced off with one another for so long that their troops became ammunition poor; Confederate soldiers were fined twenty-five cents for firing a gun without permission. The Clisby Austin house, an antebellum mansion in Tunnel Hill, doubled as a hospital during the Battle of Chickamauga; it was there that the Confederate general John B. Hood went with his severed leg, waiting to recuperate without it or be buried with it.

During the famous Battle of Missionary Ridge in November 1863, the 980-foot-long tunnel beneath the battleground became a place for soldiers to hide and fight.

Traveling through Time

One hundred years later, a different battle was won at Missionary Ridge when Robert Soule began a forty-five-year commitment to the Tennessee Valley Railroad Museum, creating a Mecca for devotees of the mechanical. If that railroad tunnel is haunted by history, it also hums with the spirit of the museum, the labor of a dedicated group of railroad enthusiasts and the lifelong dream of its founder.

Soule dreamed of creating a self-sustaining museum with a working shop to educate and entertain. The dream came true in the form of 1930s-style Grand Junction Depot, its rolling stock representing the best in the Golden Age of Steam.

A "centerpiece" of the museum is its Missionary Ridge Local—a fifty-minute trip back in time, a journey through railroad history that is carefully orchestrated from Soule's vision. Riding through the Missionary Ridge Tunnel in a historic train, passengers on the local seem to travel through time. At the East Chattanooga Back Shop, riders witness the turntable and wye, marvels of engineering that turn trains around as if they were children's toys.

The largest operating historic railroad in the South, the Tennessee Valley Railroad Museum combines the drama of Chattanooga history with the compelling tale of the era of the steam engine. From tunnel to turntable, the adventure enthralls.

TNT Plant—Volkswagen

Known to Chattanoogans as the TNT Plant, the Volunteer Army Ammunition Plant served through World War II, the Korean War and Vietnam, producing over 284 million pounds of TNT before being redesignated as Enterprise South, an industrial park on a strategic site with railroad and highway access. Woods were razed and the land hummed with machinery when the Volkswagen Group of America decided to build its North American plant in Chattanooga, Tennessee.

AUDUBON ACRES

Tucked away at the end of Sanctuary Road in East Brainerd, Chattanooga's Audubon Acres honors the Cherokee naturalist Spring Frog, who was born in the 1754 in the cabin at its center. Little Owl was the brother of the legendary chief Dragging Canoe and led one of the villages in his tribal authority. Little Owl's village headquarters was on the Chickamauga Creek and included burial grounds and remnants of earlier Creek and Mississippian villages.

Today a site that embraces nature and welcomes Chattanooga students, tourists and families, Audubon Acres is so peaceful that it's hard to imagine it as the bloody site of the separate Revolutionary War slaughters at the hands of Evan Shelby and John Sevier.

Chapter 5
GEORGIA

CHICKAMAUGA CHATTANOOGA NATIONAL BATTLEFIELD PARK

The fog, as it rolls into the Chickamauga-Chattanooga National Military Park, is thick and heavy, making sounds boom, echoing against the monuments and rustling in the dense leaves. The two-hundred-odd acres of park are heavily wooded, and the rough, rocky terrain has seen blood and anguish since the Native Americans called it "Chickamauga," or the "river of death."

The combined casualties from the battle that was waged here were more than thirty-seven thousand, 70 percent of whom died in anguish, perishing of their wounds days after the shots had stopped, many not buried until months later. And still, some casualties of the battlefield may not have left.

Spectral Soldiers

Ghosts on that land were storied even as war raged; battlefield legends cited apparitions on Snodgrass Hill at the height of the conflict. Later accounts described women keening for their lost, dead men carrying lanterns, which waved in the night's breeze.

No doubt the site's haunted reputation was renewed years later, when another wave of death marked the battlefield. During the Spanish-American War, thousands of soldiers died while encamped there, ravaged by typhoid, a plague that ran like fire through the Tennessee Valley.

The Chickamauga-Chattanooga National Battlefield Park was the first park created by the National Park Service. Its birth came from a reunion celebration of Union and Confederate soldiers.

Some stories of ghostly encounters on the battlefield are more recent. Those include reports by two park officers, Ed Tinney and Jeffrey Leathers, both of whom described weird tales of strange accidents, ghostly apparitions and eerie sounds. Tourists, visitors and neighbors still talk in low tones about the glowing eyes of the misty creatures of the night.

Mystery of Wilder Tower

The park's main monument itself holds a mystery. The majestic tower is eighty-five feet high, built by surviving members of Union general John T. Wilder's Lightning Brigade. When the men began construction in 1903, they put a cache of war memorabilia in its cornerstone, destined to be opened in the far-off year of 1976.

As that year approached, the community eagerly awaited the event. The United States' bicentennial would celebrate not only the end of a war that had bloodied the land but also the brotherly spirit that inspired former enemies to work together to build a park for future generations.

Imagine the shock when the cornerstone was revealed as empty, with no marks or evidence of forced entry!

Wilder Tower commemorates the soldiers who served under General John T. Wilder, the commander of the first assault on the city who later served as its mayor.

Formidable Fighter

The men of the Lightning Brigade had dedicated the tower to their beloved leader, a man of great character. His earliest service tested him when Confederate general Robert E. Lee's nephew was injured and Wilder, under a flag of truce, brought the young soldier's body to his grieving uncle.

Wilder was a driven and talented man. An inventor, he owned the patent on a unique water wheel, owned a forge and was a renowned expert in the field of hydraulics. He also came from a long line of soldiers; his ancestors fought in both the Revolutionary War and the War of 1812.

Wilder had been captain of his unit for a few months before being promoted to lieutenant colonel. Because of his dedication to science and his men, he gained an honorable reputation and rapidly advanced in rank, eventually becoming a regimental colonel and then general.

When the Union army asked him to lead his men to war on the backs of mules and armed with knives, he used his own money to put his men on horseback, armed with seven-shot Spencer rifles. His forge also produced two cannons in order to equip his own artillery battery. His unit's passion earned the name "the Lightning Brigade."

In a bold move, as the brigade approached Chattanooga, Wilder instructed his men to build fires over a large area in order to make the enemy believe that they were a more formidable force.

Chattanooga Legacy

Wilder's brigade was the first to enter Chattanooga, and he was formally commended for his role in the Battle of Chickamauga. He resigned due to illness in 1864, settled in Chattanooga in 1867, founded an ironworks here and served for a term as mayor of Chattanooga, his adopted city. He established a rail-manufacturing company and helped promote and construct the Charleston, Cincinnati & Chicago Railroad.

Wilder ran unsuccessfully for the United States Congress and served from 1877 to 1882 as city postmaster, later becoming commissioner of the new military park where he and his men had battled so bravely. Thirty-six years after the war, as a monument to their beloved leader, these men built a tower from which the entire battlefield can be seen—a view their leader surely would have coveted during those arduous battles, and a place where many of their descendants have since gathered to celebrate family and country.

While the legacy, landscape and lore of the land make it ripe for mystery, the spirit of brotherhood and community that inspired the creation of this, the first of our national parks, can lend a triumphant tone to the somber, sometimes spooky sounds of the forest.

LAKE WINNEPESAUKAH

Named for a Native American word meaning "bountiful waters," the Lake Winnepesaukah Amusement Park has been entertaining families for over eighty-five years. Still a family operation, Lake Winnie has the oldest mill chute water ride in the United States. The Boat Chute, built in 1926, drops into a pond with fish that are so massive they draw their own crowds. The Cannon Ball, a wooden roller coaster built in 1967, is

Lake Winnie is the name affectionately given to Lake Winnepesaukah Amusement Park, home to historic roller coasters and one of the oldest family-owned amusement parks in the United States.

2,272 feet long with a vertical drop of 70 feet, reaching speeds of up to fifty miles per hour.

Featuring an antique carousel, an entertaining midway, live music, a carnival environment and county fair–style food service, this historic park is a destination for families from all over the region.

THE JOHN ROSS HOUSE

The John Ross House remains standing, a memorial to the family who led the growth of the Chattanooga valley, linking their service to their community with their family businesses while supporting the pioneers and traders coming to the region.

William Shorey, John McDonald, Daniel Ross and John Ross were a line of men who personified the filial connections of Scottish and Cherokee heritage. They had a passion for the land and people that lifted them up as leaders in their community. Built in 1779 by John McDonald for his Cherokee wife, the John Ross house sits in what we call Rossville, on what was the head of an Indian trading path.

CHIEF WAUHATCHIE'S HOME

Chief Wauhatchie served with a company of Cherokee warriors in the War of 1812. Fighting alongside Major General Andrew Jackson and future Cherokee Chief John Ross against the Creeks, records say that Wauhatchie was severely wounded and lost his horse during the battles. Later a signer of the Hiwassee Purchase of 1817 that provided the land that became Hamilton County, Wauhatchie was listed in the U.S. Census of 1835. His home became the site of farmland as pioneers moved in during the wake of the Indian Removal Act.

LEE AND GORDON'S MILL

James Gordon came to the Chattanooga valley in 1836 and built a gristmill on the banks of the Chickamauga Creek, rebuilding it in 1857 and adding a sawmill and the first general store on the Georgia side of the valley. Union forces seized the mill from Gordon's son-in-law in 1863, taking James Morgan Lee prisoner and forcing him to supply Federal troops. The mill changed hands during the war, serving alternately as headquarters for the Confederate General Bragg and the Union General Crittendon.

Sitting between opposing forces, the mill was the site of constant skirmishes. It was burned and rebuilt by James Lee in 1867. The mill continued to operate and can be visited in the historic city of Chickamauga.

WORLD WAR I AND WORLD WAR II BARNHARDT CIRCLE

Even after it ceased to be a battlefield, having marked the second-bloodiest conflict of the Civil War, the area around Chattanooga continued to be a bulwark of our nation's defense. It served a military role through three more wars and was the site of a reconciliation that sets an example even today.

Georgia

The sights and sounds of the wooded Tennessee Valley became familiar as home to spies, future presidents, military leaders and a new breed of soldier: women called to serve their country.

Chattanooga Times founder Adolph Ochs and Civil War general John T. Wilder, men who cared deeply for their adopted city, worked tirelessly to protect the land around it, which was still tainted with the blood of their friends and neighbors. Both were instrumental in the establishment of Chickamauga-Chattanooga Battlefield as our country's first national military park, which continues to serve and teach.

Training among the Ghosts

As the twentieth century approached and the country prepared to enter yet another conflict, the Spanish-American War, legislation was passed creating forts at the various military parks in order to house and train soldiers bound for war. In 1898 a portion of the Chickamauga Chattanooga National Military Park was designated "Camp Thomas" in honor of Civil War general George H. Thomas, known as the "Rock of Chickamauga." Camp Thomas became a staging ground for soldiers preparing to leave for Cuba and Puerto Rico.

Imagine young men preparing for battle, training by charging Snodgrass Hill, listening to the ghostly whispers of the wind rustling through the park and imagining the journey before them.

Scholars and Spies

During World War I, German prisoners of war as well as German nationals living in the United States were interned at Fort Oglethorpe. Among the captives were eminent poets, scholars, businessmen, scientists, the leaders of two famous symphonies—and spies. The *New York Times*, in July 1917, reported that one prisoner at Fort Oglethorpe, the German consul general Carl Heynen, had "desired to make in this country a high explosive ammunition of the caliber that would fit guns of German design" and was credited by the American Secret Service with "being the most powerful German south of the Rio Grande."

Another prisoner, renowned physicist Jonathan Zenneck, was a pioneer in wireless technology. Along with New York banker Herr Borgemeister, Zenneck took solace in the gardens, kilns and community of the prison camp; many of the bricks these prisoners fired still can be seen in the courtyard.

"Fort O" Flourishes

Between wars, Fort Oglethorpe was a premier assignment for soldiers, who could enjoy polo matches, horse shows, parades, mock war games, concerts and officers' club dances, as well as nearby Chattanooga's vibrant social scene. The horses of the Sixth Cavalry, permanently stationed there in 1919, provided the percussion to the wind whistling in the trees and the concerts playing on the bandstands.

Some have called Chattanooga the "funnel of the universe," and Fort Oglethorpe became that for the military, with such luminaries as U.S. Army general "Black Jack" Pershing, Sergeant Alvin York and a young First Lieutenant Dwight David Eisenhower marching through its gates. Fort Oglethorpe also was home to the Third Army Women's Army Corps; thousands of WACS trained here to support the war and were reviewed by President Franklin Delano Roosevelt and the ever-handsome Bing Crosby.

Keeping a Community Spirit

Letters, newspaper reports and personal accounts of Fort Oglethorpe share a similar fond tone, whether written by soldiers departing for battle, prisoners waiting out the war or women carving a new place in service to their country. When the military base was decommissioned, the civilian leaders of the community, honoring Georgia's founder, the British army officer General James Edward Oglethorpe, formally incorporated the city of Fort Oglethorpe.

The secrets of this place carry the sounds of the past and the hope for its future. Touted as a successful example of adaptive restoration, Fort Oglethorpe continues to move forward, having transformed from a sea of wooden military barracks to a thriving city at the gateway to the Chickamauga-Chattanooga National Military Park.

PARADISE GARDENS

In an improbable world a preacher came to be at three, called by a vision of his sister, her spirit walking up the steps to heaven. The youngest in a family of thirteen children, Howard Finster carried the vision he had at age three with him. Declaring himself saved at the age of sixteen, he began sharing his religious message.

From revival tents to congregations, Reverend Finster was startled out of his pulpit of forty-five years one Sunday evening when a congregant couldn't remember his sermon. The Reverend Howard Finster would then begin a ministry that caused him to be heralded as the "grandfather of American folk art."

This man believed that "visual art is a great thing. It draws the attention of people. That's what people's work does. It preaches for them after they're gone." He had spoken to audiences of believers as a pastor for many years before he stepped away from the lectern and took up a visual ministry through art designed to last.

Father of five children, faithful husband and servant of his Lord, Finster created the Paradise Gardens Park in 1961 and was transformed in his faith by the image of a face in his fingerprint fifteen years later, drawn by a mysterious voice to do sacred art. With his characteristic fervor, he began making sacred art, immortalizing in words and form the messages that he wanted to share forever with the world.

"I took the pieces you threw away and put them together by night and day, washed by rain and dried by sun a million pieces all in one." Art in all forms is created from all kinds of recycled materials in Paradise Gardens. Summerville, Georgia, the county seat of Chattooga County, is home to the four-acre plot of land that boasts a maze of structures and sculptures.

His vision called Reverend Finster to create five thousand works of sacred art, and his fervor for this expression became so powerful that the numbered works exceeded fifty thousand before his death at age eighty-four. Messages in vivid color and words in jigsawed images exist amid the jungle of berries, fruit and the vibrant green of the north Georgia garden. There are thousands of structures and sculptures, each with its own story, message and artistic identity.

Howard Finster was an emotive man, so passionate about his role as a messenger for his Lord that he was often moved to tears sharing his ministry. He enjoyed the irony that the twenty-six verses of the Bible that he wove into the cover of a Talking Heads album reached one million people in two and a half months. Celebrating his collaboration with rock stars like Talking Heads and REM, Finster appeared on the *Tonight Show* and was featured on the cover of *TIME* magazine.

Iconic for his "outsider art," Reverend Finster was enthusiastic about other artists working in found objects and became a fan of and mentor to two Chattanooga men, Dennis Palmer and Bob Stagner, founders of the Shaking Ray Levi Society (SRLS). In a concert with instruments all created from found art, Howard heard a sound that struck a chord for him. The diminutive man found allies, comrades and students in the men who brought innovative and collaborative music and art to their city.

The SRLS is a collective-run nonprofit that supports, produces and presents diverse genres of music, film and performance art through festivals, recordings and the Internet. Since 1986, the SRLS has been dedicated to nurturing the next generation of nontraditional artists and arts advocates who will continue to challenge local audiences and enhance the cultural growth of Chattanooga, Tennessee.

Dennis and Bob continue to share the passion and prayers of the Reverend Finster as they teach children through their music, classes, art and the spirit with which they approach them all. They teach Chattanooga's youth with the same intensity that Howard taught them, preaching about personal strength and powerful art.

NEW ECHOTA

What began as the vision of one president ended as the dream of another—and was connected by Chattanooga, Tennessee. The remarkable community called New Echota, near today's Calhoun, Georgia, was the center of forbidden love, a Supreme Court battle, treacherous treaties and "blood oath" assassinations.

The Vision of Elias Boudinot

George Washington was inaugurated our country's first president on April 30, 1789. But during the nation's early years, eight other men served as president of the United States in Congress Assembled (the Continental Congress). The second of those presidents was Elias Boudinot, also president of the American Bible Society, who in 1817 supported both the birth of the Brainerd Mission, which served the Cherokee population in what is now Chattanooga. He also established the Foreign Mission School in Cornwall, Connecticut.

Two students at the Brainerd Mission School were John Ridge and Buck Watie—son and nephew of Major Ridge, a Cherokee statesman who earned his name serving with General Andrew Jackson. When the young men were invited to attend the Foreign Mission School, young Buck Watie adopted the name of the Cherokee Nation's benefactor, Elias Boudinot.

Major Ridge's visit to Cornwall was a regal affair; he arrived in a beautiful carriage, wearing garments laced with gold threads. His son and nephew also made an impression in the New England town. The young men were noted for their intellect and oratory skills, and their brilliant writings and political accomplishments were celebrated—until the men fell in love with and married two of the town's young maidens. The two couples were burned in effigy in Cornwall, but they lived peacefully in the Cherokee Nation's new capital of New Echota.

The Heart of a New Nation

There are peaceful green fields at New Echota State Park, just off of I-75 at Calhoun. But the history of that land resonates with drama and tragedy. Forbidden love, a Supreme Court battle, a treacherous president and even assassinations are part of the lore of the capital of the Cherokee Nation. A once-thriving planned town, New Echota saw the birth of a language, a government and a printing press that catapulted the Cherokee people into an educated, progressive nation within a nation.

A pioneer of that nation was George Guess, a Cherokee silversmith. A thoughtful but uneducated young man of mixed blood, he had been disabled in a hunting accident. From eighty-six characters, the man who became known as Sequoyah created a written language that the Cherokee routinely learned in three days. As a result, the love of learning and reading spread like fire through the nation of information-hungry Cherokees.

Meanwhile, white settlers were eyeing the lush lands of the Cherokee Nation and its farms and plantations, eager to win land by lottery. In 1824, John Quincy Adams won the presidency in a narrow victory over the flamboyant Andrew Jackson, who waited in the wings as the desire for rich Cherokee land inflamed white voters.

In 1827, the Cherokee Nation ratified its constitution. In 1828, the *Cherokee Phoenix* was first published, with Ridge's nephew, Elias Boudinot, as publisher and editor. The *Phoenix* spread the religious message of its patrons and the news of the day in the Nation and abroad. These milestones helped elevate the status of the Cherokee from a tribe of "savages" to a unified nation with a legitimate government charter, a capital city, a newspaper—and an enemy in the form of newly elected President Andrew Jackson.

Jackson's Dream of Indian Removal

While Andrew Jackson claimed to be a friend to the native tribes, few survived extinction to celebrate that friendship. Jackson, who had lost his own father at age fourteen, was himself the adoptive father of an orphaned Creek, and he had introduced the Cherokee to the missionaries who founded the Brainerd Mission. But after the 1828 discovery of gold in Dahlonega, Georgia, inflamed the rush to the Cherokee Nation, Jackson would lead the Cherokee out of their plentiful land on the agonizing Trail of Tears.

That mass eviction, which led to the deaths of thousands of Cherokees, happened despite the Supreme Court's landmark ruling that an Indian named Samuel Worcester could not be forcibly removed from his New Echota home. President Jackson refused to enforce the ruling, his eagerness to hasten Indians' removal to the West inspiring white raiding parties and squatters to encroach farther onto Cherokee land.

Facing broken treaties, greedy settlers and uncertain times, the Cherokee tribal council passed a "blood law" proclaiming death to anyone making treaties to dispose of tribal land without permission from the Cherokee national authorities.

The Chief John Ross House is a popular historic site in present-day Rossville and was the home of the Cherokee chief who led the nation and founded Ross's Landing, a thriving trading post that became Chattanooga.

Cherokee principal chief John Ross—the Scotsman Indian who established Ross's Landing, the future Chattanooga—opposed any treaty with the United States. Meanwhile, Major Ridge was one of a small number of Cherokee who felt that the Nation would need to relocate if it were to survive.

In 1830, President Jackson signed the Indian Removal Act, making the forced journey west inevitable. When Ridge's nephew, Elias Boudinot, began to accept his uncle's opinions about removal, John Ross censored any debate of the subject in the *Cherokee Phoenix*. Boudinot resigned in protest. Thus began a bitter schism that would continue between the Ross and Ridge factions of the Cherokee leadership.

In what he considered an act of self-preservation for the Cherokee, Major Ridge requested from the federal government a removal price of $5 million. Incensed, John Ross requested $20 million but withdrew from negotiations after President Jackson's $5 million counteroffer. An uneasy alliance between the two Cherokee factions continued until the Treaty of New Echota, by which the Ridge faction sealed the $5 million deal with the U.S. government.

Blood Oath Fulfilled

Decades earlier, the Cherokee town of Chota (in what is now Monroe County, Tennessee) was considered a safe haven for those fearing revenge under blood laws. New Echota offered no such refuge. Ridge and his followers knew that by signing the 1836 Treaty of New Echota they might save the people of the Cherokee Nation, but they would also put themselves in mortal danger.

It is a mystery whether the Treaty of New Echota and the ensuing Indian removal saved the Cherokee from extinction. The treaty certainly cost the lives of the men who signed it; their assassinations, a fulfillment of the Cherokee blood oath, began a war among the tribal factions. When the American Civil War interrupted the tribal war, Stand Watie—brother to Elias Boudinot and nephew of Major Ridge, both slain—escaped the assassins. He went on to become the last Confederate general to surrender.

DAHLONEGA

Few things get people moving like the glow of gold—especially if it's free for the taking. A few hours to our east there is a historic city that sprouted up in the shiny dust of the first gold rush in our country's history. In Dahlonega,

Georgia, the oldest courthouse in the state tells the dramatic story of the gold rush that forever changed the heart of the Cherokee Nation. Thousands of prospectors flocked into Cherokee land in north Georgia, hungry for the nuggets of coppery gold particular to that region.

Gold nuggets were found glinting in the sun among rocks and creek beds and may have been the shiny playthings of Cherokee children before the first white man made his discovery in 1829. News of the multimillion-dollar mother lode spread through the South, and men chased their dreams of riches to the heart of the Cherokee Nation, to land owned by native chiefs, tribes and families.

Land of Promise

In 1824, the ground was being laid for the Cherokee removal—now known as the Trail of Tears—and a delegation of tribal chiefs and leaders met with President James Monroe to plead for fairness for their people. Treaties were not being honored, the Cherokee people were being urged to leave their

Major Ridge earned his name fighting alongside Andrew Jackson. Major Ridge and his son, John Ridge, and nephew, Elias Boudinot, were pioneers, creating change in the Cherokee Nation.

tribal lands and a dramatic Supreme Court battle had stripped the Nation and its people of their rights, land and dignity.

That Cherokee delegation included both Chief John Ross and Major Ridge, men who were instrumental in the creation of the Brainerd Mission and what would become Chattanooga. Major Ridge had earned his title fighting in the Revolutionary War, and he played a key role in ending Chief Dragging Canoe's bloody rampage on pioneers traveling the dangerous river through Chattanooga. (One of those travelers was a child who would go on to become the wife of President Andrew Jackson.)

Having been established in 1817, the Brainerd Mission and Chattanooga were at the epicenter of ten other missions and important enough to have been visited by two presidents, James Monroe and James Madison. Staunch missionaries braved what were dense, dark forests where Eastgate Mall now sits; they were known throughout the country and England for the work they did to educate an entire nation of Cherokee people.

The missionaries' native students took their lessons of godliness and respect for the people and the world around them, enthusiastically spreading the word among tribes and nations. Ripe and bursting with the promise of their future, these students grew to be men who created a Cherokee press and newspaper at New Echota, near Calhoun, Georgia. The *Cherokee Phoenix* printed tracts that were read by a people thirsty for knowledge—and frightened by the hungry looks of encroaching squatters.

The publishers of the *Cherokee Phoenix*, Elias Boudinot and John Ridge, represented all of what was possible for the Cherokee Nation. Boudinot (Major Ridge's nephew) and John Ridge (Major Ridge's son) were among the first graduates of the Brainerd Mission and had been chosen for coveted spots at the Cornwall Mission School in Connecticut. Both young men were strong, handsome, remarkably learned, gifted with languages and statesmen driven to be catalysts in the transformation of their Nation and their people.

Land of Gold

The Cherokee Nation had a burgeoning form of government and a newspaper that was the vehicle of information, faith and inspiration. The Nation also had land and gold—the craving for which turned squatters, pioneers and politicians into savage crowds, burning Cherokee crops and looting houses, including Major Ridge's plantation near the Dahlonega gold fields.

President Andrew Jackson's first piece of legislation before a new Congress was the Indian Removal Bill. Claiming to be a friend of the Indians, Jackson was known for having "befriended" tribes now extinct; fiery Tennessee congressman Davy Crockett proposed an amendment to the bill that called for the removal of all whites from eastern Tennessee.

Cherokee tears stained the land from Chattanooga's own Ross's Landing along a death march to the West, as millions of dollars in gold were mined in the Georgia woods of Dahlonega. Today little is said in Dahlonega about its Native American heritage, but the majestic views at nearby state parks are inspiring, and the tale of early American pioneers is told in the historic district and working mines of town.

When Major Ridge, a veteran of wars, leader of people and peer of presidents, learned that gold had been discovered on his land, it is easy to imagine that he smiled, envisioning how the good fortune could help his people. He was convinced that the Cherokee Nation could survive only if they sold the land, fetching a good price from the U.S. government before the Nation was driven from it altogether.

Little did Ridge know that his story would end in assassination; his death was ordered according to the "blood law" pact signed by chiefs declaring it treason to cede land without tribal permission. Major Ridge, his son John and nephew Elias were assassinated, some while their wives slept, for their earlier trust in America's leaders and legal system.

Chapter 6

SIGNAL MOUNTAIN

SIGNAL MOUNTAIN

Developed by Charles E. James, the Signal Mountain community was originally developed as a hunting club atop Walden's Ridge, a two-thousand-foot-high ridge on the southern tip of Signal Mountain. Charles was the son of the reverend Jesse J. James, who came to Chattanooga in 1854 and was a guiding force behind the 1919 charter of the City of Signal Mountain. One of the first millionaires in the city, Charles James was famous for the James Building, a skyscraper when it was built on Broad Street. James was a driving force behind the inclines traversing both Signal and Lookout Mountains.

Interpretive signs for the Civil War Trails system guide motorists along the same switchbacks and sharp turns that soldiers may have used when the Signal bluffs were stations to signal corpsmen of both armies as Chattanooga and its lookouts changed hands with the fortunes of war.

ANDERSON TURNPIKE/THE W ROAD

Its turns and switchbacks perched perilously up Signal Mountain, the Anderson Turnpike was an already established path up the steep mountain when the Union troops arrived in Chattanooga. During the famous Wheeler's Raid, led by the Confederate cavalry leader against Union General Thomas's troops, it became legendary for the circle of fire seen as the wagons burned.

The W Road, known for its sharp switchbacks, was called the Anderson Turnpike, and portions are still in use today.

A portion of the turnpike was later called the W Road for the three hairpin turns that were constructed in the absence of a natural break in the mountain, an engineering feat that remains relevant and usable today.

SIGNAL MOUNTAIN SPACE HOUSE

Chattanooga is a charmed place to be a child today, but can you imagine the fervor among Chattanooga's children thirty-five years ago, when the Space House was being built on Signal Mountain?

Newspaper reports in 1973 estimated that twenty to thirty thousand cars made the drive to the infamous switchback curve to see a sight that can still thrill people who aren't expecting it. (It's hard not to catch your breath when you see what appears to be a flying saucer seemingly parked on the side of a lush, green mountain.) Back then, Chattanooga's children must have felt like Mickey Mouse was eating Pop Rocks right next door with the Loch Ness Monster and Bigfoot. The stories that circulated on playgrounds and schoolyards during those years must have grown even more believable as the *E.T.* phenomenon burned through theaters and imaginations all over the country.

A Saucer with a View

Its builder, C.W. King, called it a "House of the Twenty-first Century" and placed it on three-quarters of an acre of land with a view of the Tennessee River. When it was built, the unusual house was celebrated by the Electric Power Board as an all-electric home, and King hoped the inspiring design would be the prototype for a new boom in the building industry.

The first real estate agent to hold the listing for what locals began calling the "Space House" recalled her experience in a 2007 article in the *Times Free Press*. She described an event that drew so many cars that "the police showed up to do traffic control." Planned as a three-hour tour, the open house lasted into the night and ended with a latecomer trying to climb up the retractable stairs as they were closing, desperate for a peek inside the strange house.

Super Space-ious

Inside, the Space House is larger than it looks. The legs of the house support the steel-and-concrete structure and contain the electrical and plumbing connections to the remarkably spacious saucer that is a three-level home. The almost two thousand square feet of living space has been featured in several national television shows and has drawn media interest repeatedly during the decades that it has perched on the side of the mountain.

As a "House of the Twenty-first Century," the Space House remains a beacon that still guides families with out-of-state tags up the switchbacks of Signal Mountain so that their children can take pictures of one of the most unusual homes in the country. It has changed hands several times in the last few years, and its price has fluctuated. But it has drawn steady interest from people both here and abroad. Dozens braved tempestuous March thunderstorms to see the house when it was auctioned recently— some disappointed that there weren't souvenirs, but all thrilled to have had the opportunity to tour an iconic part of the Tennessee Valley's landscape.

The new owner prefers to remain anonymous. She is known only as an Ohio woman who won the house at the March 15 auction, with a telephoned bid of $135,000; the details of her purchase are not yet on record with the Hamilton County Courthouse. The mystery of her identity is just another one of the secrets of the Space House.

Chapter 7

NORTH OF CHATTANOOGA

RED CLAY COUNCIL GROUND

Chief John Ross and his guest, John Howard Payne (author of *Home Sweet Home*), were arrested from his Red Clay home and imprisoned in Georgia on November 7, 1835. The Red Clay Council Ground was site of the last Cherokee Council before the Indian removal called the Trail of Tears began.

Today the site celebrates the Cherokee Nation and its heritage. It is part of the National Park System and a place where families can learn to embrace the past while looking toward the future.

CHATATA

Was there a charlatan at Chatata, or was this outpost of Chattanooga the last stop of the two lost tribes of Israel? In fits and bursts, a father and his son uncovered a wall in Bradley County forest in what is now Red Clay State Park. The discoveries were scientific sensations, and twice—in both 1821 and 1920—the media flocked to our valley to report on this national curiosity.

This seven-hundred-foot wall appeared to be just an oddly regular outcropping of rocks—until a farmer, Isaac Hooper, dug more deeply. In 1891, the *Cleveland Herald* described Hooper's find. The wall, it reported, had "three tiers of stone in which the strange characters appeared only on the west face of the middle tier."

The Smithsonian Institution displayed a portion of the stone from the Chatata Wall from 1900 to 1902 before returning it to the property owners. In the coming decades, there were varying "translations" of the characters, suggesting that our lush valley and rolling hills once held not only the imprints of the moccasins worn by the earliest Americans but also the imprints of the soles of the wandering tribes of Israel.

Unearthing a Mystery

Our valley is a land of families, traditions and the passing on of property. Isaac Hooper inherited his Bradley County land from a succession of generations of Hooper men, their families growing strong amid the slopes of the farmlands and forests, surviving the lean years of the post-Reconstruction South.

For generations, Hooper men had cultivated the soil; so, eventually, it was Isaac Hooper's son who resurrected his father's discovery. Now a farmer like his ancestors, moving rocks to till that land, he found a stone marker that didn't make sense to him.

Wavy lines, said to depict travel overseas, drawings of kangaroos and depictions of the moon and several stars are among the wall's markings, as described by the *Chattanooga Times* in 1920. The article also chronicled the visits to the Chatata Wall by historians from New Zealand, Italy, Japan, Cuba, France and Spain.

Digging Deeper into History

Albert Leighton Rawson, a New York professor who was visiting the area, heard tell of the stone with the strange markers. As fate would have it, he was the man who had achieved fame deciphering the Moabite stone, a historical treasure that sparked a generation of early Indiana Jones types. Rawson was a writer, a member of the Brotherhood of Lebanon and a scholar of the Druzes of Mount Lebanon, an early incarnation of the group that would become the Knights of the Templar, or members of Masonic Temples.

Rawson was known for organizing outdoor religious meetings set among areas of striking natural beauty, notably the 1878 Watkins Glen Freethinkers Convention. One can imagine that the allure of the Tennessee Valley and the unique meroglyphics that Rawson identified on the Chatata Wall created great excitement in both scientific and media outlets.

Quoting Deuteronomy, the professor maintained that the writings told of the lost tribes of Israel, drawn to this valley and compelled to follow the injunction of Moses and carve the scripture of their fathers on great stones with plaster. Though there were whispers of fakery, records indicate that Rawson financed the reputed $35,000 excavation himself, and parts of the wall are rumored to remain in the possession of the descendants of the Hooper family.

The Buried Secret

Sadly, as with many mysteries, we may never know the truth about the Chatata Wall. As is often the case, scientific advances came too late to solve its riddles, relegating them to the files of questions we haven't answered. Even at the time of the wall's discovery, experts couldn't agree on the markings' meaning; some saw connections to the early language of Sequoyah, others to ancient Hebrew.

Markings of a similar nature were found in New Mexico, seemingly having been there for eons. Over the years there were many attempts to translate them using various languages; only in this era were they identified as being from the Phoenician-Greek alphabet used in 500 BC.

Whether or not the whispers we hear are from travelers from our prehistory, the beauty of the land surrounding the Red Clay State Park is a testament to what nature offers us in this Tennessee Valley.

LOST SEA

Ben Sands grew up hearing stories about a magnificent underground lake. Pioneers in the area around Sweetwater, Tennessee, had been weaving stories around Craighead Caverns since they came to settle there in 1820. Named for its earliest owner, the Cherokee chief Craighead, the caverns were central to local lore, fables from Cherokee history mixing with Civil War tales, spy intrigue, saltpeter mining and pioneering power. Young Ben often entered the caverns along with his father, who guided groups hunting for arrowheads there.

In 1905, thirteen-year-old Ben was exploring the caves on his own when he ventured farther than ever before. Pushing past a shallow pool in a familiar chamber, he crawled through a small underwater opening in the chamber wall to emerge in a vast, dark cavern with a lake so large that he couldn't find its end. The young boy threw mud balls in every direction, hoping to find the edge of the amazing lake—but he heard only splashes and the echo of his efforts. Ben wouldn't know for decades that he had discovered the largest underground lake in the United States, the second largest in the world—a four-and-a-half-acre body of water three hundred feet beneath the earth's surface.

Imagine that young explorer's joy as he returned to his family and classmates to share his discovery! History comes alive for explorers, whatever their ages. To young Ben, when he made his awesome discovery, the shadows in that marvelous lake room must have danced with the ghosts of the Cherokee councils, Union spies and Confederate miners who had been there years before. The skepticism of adults, plus droughts that caused the pool to fluctuate, kept people from believing Ben's story about a "lost sea" for years.

In 1915, with Prohibition coming, a developer purchased the caverns, creating a dance floor, tavern and entertainment venue in the series of caves, some already occupied by moonshiners.

Earlier "Cave Men"

Relics, pottery, weapons and jewelry bear testament to the Cherokee use of the caverns as an important meeting site, and the massive tracks of a giant Pleistocene jaguar tell a tale of a five-hundred-pound animal that lost its way in the caves over twenty thousand years ago. In the 1820s, pioneers took advantage of the caverns' constant fifty-eight-degree temperature to store their roots and vegetables.   During the Civil War, the caves were a critical source of the saltpeter necessary for the manufacture of gunpowder. Diaries from the era reveal the critical importance that mining in the caves played in the war effort. One diary entry tells the tale of a Union spy, caught and shot trying to blow up the cave's entrance to keep valuable saltpeter from the guns of Confederate soldiers.

Scientists have confirmed that some initials on the cave walls were "painted" with the carbon of a soldier's torch—providing another layer of authentic 1863 history hundreds of feet underground. The Confederate soldiers who volunteered for the dangerous duty of distributing the gunpowder were legendary for their courage, and the miners were known among soldiers for working days and nights without sleep to keep the Confederate guns blazing with Tennessee Valley saltpeter.

From the 1920s to the 1960s, the caverns became home to several businesses that created more connections to Sweetwater's southern neighbor, Chattanooga. Manure from Fort Oglethorpe's Sixth Cavalry fed a mushroom farm in the caverns in the 1930s, and the Tennessee Power Company, a Chattanooga creation, installed a revolutionary lighting system in Craighead Caverns during the 1920s. With its holding building in what we now know as Parkway Towers (the blight at the edge of Finley Field), the Tennessee Power Company worked with farmers in the rural Sweetwater area to cut poles and provide the right of ways that brought them electric service.

Ben's "Lost Sea" Rediscovered

Ben Sands was an old man when the underground lake in Craighead Caverns was rediscovered; he was honored as its first official visitor and was asked to name it. More than fifty years had passed, but the amazing lake Ben called the "Lost Sea" was finally found, and it became a leading attraction in the Tennessee Valley, drawing visitors from around the world.

Since its rediscovery, divers have measured and explored the Lost Sea. The surface of the lake measures 800 feet long and 220 feet wide, and the water is home to ghostly monsters, trout that have grown to several feet long and have lost much of their color in their habitat 300 feet under the earth's surface.

Now, tour boats skim the spooky surface of the Lost Sea, gliding past amazing rock formations, dancing lights and other fascinating sights that tell the tale every child wants to hear: wondrous discoveries can still be made, and our valley is a great place to make them.

BIBLIOGRAPHY

Armstrong, Z. *The History of Hamilton County and Chattanooga, Tennessee.* Johnson City, TN: Overmountain Press, 1931.

Arnold, D.W. *America's Trail of Tears.* Chattanooga, TN: Chattanooga Historical Foundation Co., 2005.

———. *Old Money, New South: The Spirit of Chattanooga.* Chattanooga, TN: Chattanooga Historical Foundation Co., 2006.

Bierce, A. *Civil War Stories.* New York: Dover Publications, Inc., 1994.

Broadwater, R.P. (1998). *Daughters of the cause: women of the civil war.* Altoona, PA: Daisy Publications.

Coleman, C.K. *Strange Tales of the Dark and Bloody Ground.* Nashville, TN: Rutledge Hill Press, 1998.

Fults, M.E. *Chattanooga Chills.* Chattanooga, TN: Mark E. Fults, 2006.

Furbee, M.R. *Outrageous Women of Civil War Times.* Hoboken, NJ: John Wiley & Sons, Inc., 2003.

Govan, G.E., and J.W. Livingood, J.W. *The Chattanooga Country 1540–1976.* Knoxville: University of Tennessee Press, 1977.

Green, J. *Contrary to Popular Belief.* New York: Broadway Books, 2005.

Jameson, W.C. *Buried Treasure of the South.* Little Rock, AR: August House Publishers, Inc., 1992.

Mott, A.S. *Ghost Stories of Tennessee.* Auburn, WA: Lone Pine Publishing International, 1975.

Nicely, M. *Chattanooga Walking Tour & Historic Guide.* Chattanooga, TN: Stillhouse Hollow Press, 2005.

Wangler, C. *Ghost Stories of Georgia.* Auburn, WA: Lone Pine Publishing International, 1974.

Williams, T. *Always Paddle Your Own Canoe: The Life, Legend and Legacy of Anna Safley Houston.* Chattanooga, TN: James Thomas Williams III, 1994.

Wilson, J. *Chattanooga's Story.* Chattanooga, TN: Chattanooga News-Free Press, 1980.

ABOUT THE AUTHOR

J ennifer Ley Crutchfield has always celebrated Chattanooga history. As an
army kid, hometown was the soft taste of a MoonPie, crisp refreshment
of a Coca-Cola or history leaping from library books on bases in the United
States and Latin America.

Jennifer graduated from the University of Maryland, returning to
Chattanooga as an adult. She publishes the *Chattanooga Parent Magazine* and
is a relocation agent for IOR Global Services and Volkswagen employees on
international reassignments.

Jennifer and her sons—Will, George and Max—enjoy being part of the
Chattanooga community, Northside Presbyterian Church and Normal Park
Museum Magnet Schools. They chase mysteries, learn and enjoy the family
attractions, entertainment and natural wonders of the region and the lessons
of its history.

Visit us at
www.historypress.net